MISSION
AND
SCHOOL EDUCATION

The Role of Christian Mission School Education
in Transforming Mizo Society
(1894–1952)

MISSION AND SCHOOL EDUCATION

The Role of Christian Mission School Education
in Transforming Mizo Society
(1894–1952)

J. Lalduhawma

2021

Mission and School Education: The Role of Christian Mission School Education in Transforming Mizo Society (1894–1952) - Published by the Indian Society for Promoting Christian Knowledge (ISPCK), Post Box 1585, Kashmere Gate, Delhi-110006.

Online order: http://ispck.org.in/book.php

Also available on amazon.in

ISBN: 978-93-90569-23-6

Laser typeset by

ISPCK, Post Box 1585, 1654, Madarsa Road, Kashmere Gate, Delhi-110006 • *Tel:* 23866323

e-mail: ashish@ispck.org.in • ella@ispck.org.in
website: www.ispck.org.in

Dedicated to

My parents
J. Rochunga & K. Sangzuali,
My wife
Lalrengpuii,
My children
Caleb Vanmalsawma Jinhlawng,
Sarah Lalruatsaki Jinhlawng,
Rosangpuii Jinhlawng

Contents

Acknowledgements

I am grateful to God for allowing me to publish this book, which is the outcome of my MTh (History of Christianity) thesis, submitted in March 2011 at the United Theological College Bangalore.

I express my gratitude to the Baptist Church of Mizoram for deputing me and sponsoring me during my studies as well as granting my travel expenses for doing research work from Bangalore to Mizoram.

I express my heartfelt thanks to my thesis guide, Rev. Dr. George Oomen, who motivated me in writing on this topic. He encouraged me and molded me in my academic thinking, in my zeal for doing research, and in articulating the sources and ideas with proper methodology (historiography). I regret publishing this book without his forwarding letter as I failed to reach out to him.

My thanks go to Marina Ngursangzeli Behera, Head of Department, History of Christianity UTC, Bangalore, who offered tremendous care and other contributions during our course of study. I am truly indebted to her.

Though a new version for publication has been completed, I am deeply indebted to Mrs. C. Lalrempuii, who proofread my thesis and helped me correct my English during the submission of the thesis in 2011.

I am deeply thankful to my wife, Lalrengpuii, who was caring for a newborn baby at the time but has always unceasingly supported me from those days until today.

I express my thanks to my classmates Rev. B. Zohmangaiha and Rev. Shiveraj Mahenra. They were valuable friends during our MTh studies. I am grateful we could stand by each other and encourage each other.

I am also grateful to Rev. Dr. Hrankhuma, former Professor of SAIACS, who wrote the Foreword for this book.

J. Lalduhawma

Foreword

I am very grateful to write a Foreword for this book. It is noteworthy that Christian missions have tremendously contributed to the education of many people groups around the world, reducing many languages into written form and providing the first literature to the people. The English missionaries who came to Mizoram over a century ago communicated the Gospel of Jesus Christ along with education that eventually transformed the people. The missionaries not only reduced the Mizo language into written form, providing the script and the first literature, they controlled the education in Mizoram for many years.

In my study of the changes of Mizo culture within approximately a hundred years and the factors that contributed to the changes, I found that there are four major factors that contributed to the changes; namely, the British administration of the land, Christian missions that include education, the two World Wars and the independence of India. In the midst of the rapid and drastic changes, education played an acculturative role that has been very helpful for the Mizos to adjust to the new situation rather smoothly.

One of the greatest needs of many tribal groups in India is sustainable all-round development. Education is one of the most effective factors that will help in transforming the less fortunate people groups in India. This book provides an example of the significance of education for the overall transformation of peoples. May God stimulate every reader for the blessing of India.

Rev. Dr. Fanai Hrangkhuma

Abbreviations

BCM	Baptist Church of Mizoram
Comp.	Compiler
Ed.	Editor
ff	following pages
Gov't	Government
n.d,	No year of Publication
n.p.	No place of publication given.
No	number
op.cit. *(opero citato)*	in the work cited (a work previously cited in the same research report)
trans.	Translated by
YMA	Young Mizo Association

Introduction

Christianity in Mizoram has generally been considered to have had a significant impact on Mizo society. Consequently, what needs to be considered is whether there was a change in the value systems with regard to the socioreligious, cultural, and civic spheres due to mission school education in the early years of Christianity in Mizoram.

The pioneering mission—the Arthington Aborigine Mission—came to Mizoram in 1894. A millionaire called Robert Arthington of Leeds, England, who heard about the hill people, whom the Gospel had not reached, started this missionary society. Arthington eager to preach the Gospel to these people, organized his own missionary society, called "The Arthington Aborigines Mission." On January 11, 1894, J.H. Lorraine and F.W. Savidge, members of High Gate Baptist Church in London, arrived in Aizawl to be a pioneer missionary to Mizoram under the Arthington Aborigine Mission.

After working for almost 4 years (January 1894–end of December 1897) in Mizoram, they had to leave Mizoram on the instruction of the Mission Board that sponsored them. Robert Arthington, the founder of the Mission, urged them to turn to other unreached regions by the Gospel. Meanwhile, the Welsh Calvinistic Methodist Mission adopted Mizoram as part of their mission field. Subsequently, their first missionary to Mizoram Rev. D.E. Jones arrived at Aizawl on August 30, 1897, followed by Rev. Edwin Rowlands in 1898. Thus, The Arthington Aborigine Mission was continued by the Welsh Calvinistic Methodist (later Presbyterian) Mission.

The Baptist Missionary Society (BMS) Home Committee then negotiated with the Welsh Mission who agreed to the coming of the BMS into Mizoram to work in the southern areas. The BMS invited Savidge and Lorraine to return to Mizoram as BMS missionaries, which they accepted. In 1903, the first two pioneer missionaries of the Arthington Aborigine Missionaries came back again to the southern part of Mizoram sent by the BMS London. Lorraine and Savidge arrived in Lunglei, the new BMS station on March 30, 1903.

In due course, these two missions undertook the mission work throughout the region. Both missions took up their mission work through evangelization, ecclesiastical and educational means. School education played an important role in the Christian mission work in Mizoram.

There appears to have been rapid changes in Mizo society in lifestyle and perception of religious matter along with Christianization. In general, the value system of the Mizos in terms of the sociocultural and religious and civic sense was changing during this process. Most of the writers of Christianity in Mizoram give credit to evangelization, church activities, and revival as the factors responsible for these changes. However, educational involvement has been a major component shall be looked in depth to see whether it has influenced the shaping of the value system of the Mizos.

Before establishing formal education, the missionaries had introduced nonformal education in the absence of a structural syllabus and proper school buildings. Education significantly impacted the social, cultural, and religious sphere of Mizo society. Could the system of education, the syllabus, and the policy of mission education be the sources that brought about changes in certain value systems of those Mizo who were educated in these mission schools subsequently leading to changes in the value system in the rest of Mizo society? This would be the focus of the book.

Chapter 1

The Indigenous System of Education in Mizoram

Mizoram, which was known as the Lushai Hills District till 1954, is presently one of the states in India. By an Act of the Parliament, the name Lushai Hills was changed to "Mizo District" in September 1954.[2] It is a land of hills situated in the Northeast corner of India. Education was formally introduced in 1894. However, education cannot be limited to the formally institutionalized structure. Indeed, even before the introduction of a formal framework of education, each society developed a significant and specific way of passing knowledge from one generation to the other. The values and skills of the Mizo community were nurtured and sustained through forms of traditional education that were exceptionally much portion of their social life.

The main focus of this chapter is to draw out the traditional system of education among the Mizos before the well setup of formal education in Mizoram. In dealing with the traditional system of education, an attempt is made to answer—what are the sources and resources of traditional education? How did the Mizos gather their knowledge? What was the content of education and how were the socioreligious and cultural values imparted among the Mizos? The aim is also to see how and whether those values continue and how it influences the formal education in the subsequent chapters.

1. Mizo Traditional Institution of Education

There was no formal system of education in the primitive Mizo society before 1894. However, there was a system of informal education through which the Mizo accumulated their knowledge, imparting certain value systems with reference to socioreligious and civic sense. Traditional education was basically concerned with imparting basic skills and knowledge to every person for their self-sustenance and to be a responsible member of the welfare of the community as well.

In traditional Mizo society, the kind of instruction given was centering on to meet their ground reality, hence moral, ethic, handicrafts, sports, discipline, singing and dancing, defense, customs, the art of warfare, and hunting were learned in their own context.[3] Each of these played a valuable role and contributed to the Mizo acculturation process. These were instructed through family at home and through the traditional institution called the *Zawlbuk* (Bachelor's dormitory) through old stories and folktales and additionally through other maxims and truisms. The informal modules or contents of the *Zawlbuk* education included civic duties, community ethics, defense, culture, discipline, oral history, and music. The intention was to prepare young people to become responsible citizens in society.

Zawlbuk: Meaning and Origin

Literally, the word *Zawlbuk* is a combination of two words *Zawl* and *Buk*; *Zawl implies* "flat" and *Buk* means "temporary house," thus, its literal meaning could be "house on a level ground."

However, instead of its literal connotation, it is understood in connection to its function, in fact, *Zawlbuk* is (was) "young men's dormitory" or "The Bachelors' house." J.H. Lorrain, one of the pioneer missionaries to Mizoram explains in his dictionary: "*Zawlbuk* is a large house in a Lushai village where all the unmarried young men of the community sleeps at night. It was also used as a center of training children and adolescents about good morality and behavior for a community life."[4]

N. Chatterji, an earlier senior research officer of Mizoram, rightly observed when he remarks *Zawlbuk* is, in any case, much deeper in its significances than what can be understood from such a literal meaning. It was not only the place where young men slept together but also a place where youth shaped their moral conduct and trained to be a responsible person in their society.[5] *Zawlbuk* was usually situated in the center of the village near the Chief's house.[6] Some villages, which were large and divided into several parts known as *Vengs*, have more than one *Zawlbuk*. Each *Veng* had its own *Zawlbuk* in a big village.

The origin of the *Zawlbuk* in the Mizo Society is difficult to trace as there was no written record. One common interpretation is that the Mizos might have settled within the present land in approximately 17th century by driving out the *Kuki* and other tribes. The foremost likely reason for the movement of the Mizos from the Chin Hills to the present settlement was due to frequent raids by the *Pawi's* tribes like *Zahau, Hualngo*, and *Tlang* of Falam (Myanmar).[7] K. Zawla, one of the Mizo writers, opines that in the late 18th century, *Zawlbuk* was already well set up when the Mizo occupied the present settlement.[8] This implies that the Mizo have had the institution of *Zawlbuk* as early as the 18th century. Lalbiakthanga, who did an empirical study on this area, also believes that *Zawlbuk* was introduced in the Mizo society only after they entered into the present settlement.[9] H. L. Malsawma too states that the institution of *Zawlbuk* appears at first in Khawnglung village at the time of the North–South war in Mizoram around 1860 AD.[10] Indeed in spite of the fact that there is no written record on the origin of *Zawlbuk,* it can be concluded that *Zawlbuk* was well set up when the Mizos settled within the display settlement in the early 18th century.

The Educational Significance of the *Zawlbuk*

In fact, the main reason for the existence of the *Zawlbuk* was certainly for a village defense purpose.[11] It was in the *Zawlbuk* that about the village invasion and headhunting were discussed and made a plan. In its development, the *Zawlbuk* became the center of learning in the primitive Mizo society. It is interesting to cite the comment made by the Herbert Anderson, the former Indian Secretary of the BMS, Calcutta. He said that "even before formal organized school was established among the Mizos, the *Zawlbuk* institution had already imparted a beautiful manner of obedience and respect of elders among the young Mizo."[12] N.E. Parry, earlier superintendent of Lushai Hills, also expressed his observation on the *Zawlbuk* giving a positive and remarkable comment saying that *Zawkbuk* is "an Institution with an excellent discipline, it is the center of the village life."[13] N.Chatterji also rightly regarded it as "the crucible wherein the Mizo youth, the marginal man was shaped into the responsible adult member of their society."[14] Thus, it is evidence from the comment made by the non-Mizo that the function of *Zawlbuk* played a significant role in educational field in the primitive Mizo society. Let us briefly look how *Zawlbuk* functions as the education center.

First, *Zawlbuk* was a place where they gathered knowledge. In spite of the fact that *Zawlbuk* was basically a sleeping place for young people of the village, as often as possible the old ones would visit at night sitting by the *Zawlbuk* fire and share their past experiences. They would describe their past story of hunting, war, and village life; they performed a valuable obligation in teaching and shaping the young ones.[15] It is interesting to note that it was in the *Zawlbuk* that J.H. Lorrain, the pioneer missionary of the Mizoram, made his first addressed to the group of Mizos in 1896. He says,

> My first Address on Lushai Hills 16th Sept 1896. After leaving the Chief's house, we went to the *Zawlbuk* or bachelor's quarter.—Huge fire in the center-young fellows round fires all lying on the floor smoking-or in groups about the place telling stories…Then the oldest said that they wished us to tell them a story as they had heard that we know so many Lushai fables…So after a bit I proposed that I should tell them a TRUE STORY about the way in which the world was made…[16]

This remark made by one of the first missionaries reflects that *Zawlbuk* was a place where they gathered knowledge, tell stories and tales. Every night they would share with one another either good or bad news that happened during the day in the village and also any other matter of interest.[17] Information was given and received with regard to the news of the village as well as of the other villages brought by travelers. The men travelers usually slept in the *Zawlbuk*.[18] It was in the *Zawlbuk* that recreational activities were organized by the young men. It was the place where the young men take advice with one another for undertaking any join enterprises.[19]

Second, *Zawlbuk* was a place where the young ones and children learned sports. Several kinds of indoor games were organized in the *Zawlbuk*, of which wrestling was a common game. It was the place where the young villagers learned technique of war, fighting, wrestling, singing, dancing, oratory, games and sport, handicrafts, good manners, traditions, customs, etiquette, religion, and all the essential things for their life in their own context.[20] Wrestling was obligatory for all the inmates and the smaller boys were first made to wrestle among themselves.[21] Strong wrestlers challenge up the line till they could be able to wrestle the village champion.[22]

Third, it was a place where the young ones received cultural values and civic sense, Mizo code of ethic, history of the Mizos, and skill of hunting and war from the elders by means of oral teaching.

Other than oral education, they too received practical work lesson. All the boys, earlier to coming to adolescence, had to come to *Zawlbuk* from their respective homes to work. They were anticipated to do any work the young men inquired them to do. One of the obligatory works for the bigger boys in the village was collecting woods each day for making fire in the *Zawlbuk*. Every evening, all the boys were called up for a roll call in order to proof whether all the boys do the task assigned to them. In case, anyone failed to submit one bundle of firewood, he must collect three or five bundles of firewood for disciplinary action.[23] Thus, the village boys were trained to be responsible in their duties.

Discipline was strictly enforced in the *Zawlbuk*, interference of outsiders in its administration was not acceptable. If any boy complains to his father that he has been ill-treated by the monitors and if the boy's parents in consequence beaten or abused the monitor, all the inmates of the *Zawlbuk* united to rebuff the father of the sneak. They will go to the offender's house and sit on the floor, capturing hold of the posts and shake the entire house. This punishment is aiming to show the man that they have no regard for him and do not care if he migrates to another village.[24] Parents barely counterchallenge the attitude of the inmates of the *Zawlbuk*, rather they urge their children to follow the instructions.

The Educational Function of the *Val Upa*

Zawlbuk was under the overall authority of the chief of the village. The fact that the *Zawlbuk* was almost situated at the central place in the village and very near to the chief's house, which signifies the importance of the *Zawlbuk* in the villages.[25] Indeed in spite of the fact that the *Zawlbuk* was under the overall authority of the chief, it was placed specifically under the charge of *Val Upa*,[26] the man who was the foremost efficient organizer as well as the most bold and skilled hunter among the group.[27]

The chief exercised his authority through his *Val Upa*. The *Val Upa* was responsible for the deliberate conduct of the young men. The instruction of the *Val Upa* in all matters was to be considered. The *Zawlbuk* administration would not allow any impedance of parents in connection with the discipline of the youth and boy. As Chatterji rightly said, the status of the *Val Upa* could be the same status with the superintendent of a modern public school with his/her responsibilities.[28] They ought to organize for all the social work to be done by the young men such as digging grave, carrying sick people, or any other work, which are necessary. Special arrangement is made for fetching water at night, in case the inmate of the *Zawlbuk* gets thirsty and boys were expected to do this. The boys had to supply water to the bachelors in the *Zawlbuk*.[29] Asking water from the house nearby *Zawlbuk* was understood as normal in such case the householders must not refuse to give water.

Strict unwritten rules were enforced in the *Zawlbuk* for the effective and smooth functioning of the institution. K. Thanzauva pointed out some unwritten rules in the *Zawlbuk*, which are cited below[30]:-

- Drinking rice beer or drunkenness was not allowed.
- Interference of outsiders in its administration was forbidden.

- Entering in *Zawlbuk* was prohibited for the girls.
- Stealing of any article, big, or small was regarded as very disgraceful. The disciplinary action for such a crime was a fine of Rs. 40, which one person in those periods could only earn in 100 days or more.
- Throwing a stone at the wall or roof of the *Zawlbuk* was strictly restricted. No one must throw a stone at the *Zawlbuk* for any reason. However, the chief of the village had the right to do that for certain reasons.
- The junior must obey and respect the elders.
- All inmates should constantly keen on any emergency even war.

The *Zawlbuk* inmates were divided into three groups, the *Val Upa* (senior bachelor), the *Tlangval* (young men), and the *Thingnawi fawm* (the boys). Most of the inmates of the *Zawlbawk* were unmarried, however, the young married men also slept in the *Zawlbuk* before they had one or two children.[31] The *Val Upa (s)* were the decision-maker to transfer of a member from the boys to the adult group.[32] Even though the *Val Upa* was entrusted with the authority to make the decisions, he does not seem to have abused his authority. There was a rule for peculiar testing for a boy who aspired to be promoted to the adult group.

When a boy physically grew up and had come to the age of adolescence, the young men inspected the hair of the boy's pubic area, which was pulled out by a boy from their pubic area. The pubic hair must be as long enough to tie around the stem of a Mizo bamboo-smoking pipe (1–1.5 cm in diameter) to be classed as a *Tlangval* (a young bachelor). No boys were accepted to be classed as an adult unless he passed the test.[33] On coming to the status of *Tlangval*, a boy can be exempted from collecting firewood for the *Zawlbuk*.[34] The Mizo boys were eagerly looking forward to becoming a status of *Tlangval* as they were also eagerly waiting for the time of exemption from collecting firewood for *Zawlbuk* every day.

However, in exceptional case, the *ValUpa* had the right to exercise his power in conceding a boy to the status of *Tlangval*. In case, the boy who candidates himself to examine his pubic hair but failed in the test several times, it is the *Val Upa*, who took action to help the boy in securing the boy's self-esteem and unfortunate defamatory for the group as a whole.[35] N.E Parry also observed that the *Zawlbuk* provided for the psychological needs of the boy in relation to his peers.[36] In one way, the function of the *Val Upa*, was important as the present children psychologists or good teachers in building up the self-esteem, the confidence of the children in the ground reality in those days.

Primarily, the *Zawlbuk* served as a dormitory for young men, where even married men slept. The younger men were assigned harder work such as digging graves, and carrying the sick from the *Jhum*, the work place, or even out of the jungle. They responded to *Val Upa's* orders to work wherever the need arose.[37] As mentioned earlier, the boys were given compulsory assignments of collecting firewood. They were responsible for the supply of firewood for the *Zawlbuk*. The "*Val Upa*" appointed a number of monitors who were known as *Thingnawi fawm hotu*. Monitors had to see that the boys collected sufficient firewood every day for the *Zawlbuk*. As mentioned earlier, if anyone was failing in collecting the firewood, the youth would punish the boy by giving a double task for the next day.

The monitors were appointed to maintain discipline in the *Zawlbuk* with regard to control the boys' activities and to meet the requirement of the villagers. The Mizo village life depended on the voluntary social service of the villagers. There were times when the villagers ought to contribute their service for the welfare of the village like—when there is a need to make footpaths between villages, between the cultivated lands and to water well, construction of the widows' house, etc. Each member was in need of another in several circumstances and specific emergency. Amid the night, the monitors would watch the village roads and give a signal in case any crises emerge.[38] The monitors enjoyed a good deal of power over the boys; they did not need to do any of the ordinary *Zawlbuk* work. They had the freedom to decide how to fulfill their obligation. Thus, *Zawlbuk* was the teaching and learning center in the traditional Mizo community. The institution of *Zawlbuk* could be claimed as the heart of the traditional Mizo community.

There is no proper written evidence for how and why such an institution had vanished from the Mizo society. There was no restriction from the authority of the government even the superintendent made effort to protect and keep up it.[39] J.M. Llyod said that the primary school replaced the *Zawlbuk*.[40] While Thanzauva opines that due to the British administration and the emergence of the Christian Church, the institution of *Zawlbuk* came to an end.[41]

Subsequently, the sociocultural advancement or changes due to distinctive components like British administration, the development of the churches, and the introduction of the formal school were the factors responsible for the end of the *Zawlbuk* institution. One of the important functions of *Zawlbuk* was for the safety of the village from their enemy as the primitive Mizo society frequently raids each other. Then after the British enters Mizoram's practice of raiding came to an end and thus the significance of *Zawlbuk* in the society declined and subsequently came to an end.

One of the major limitations of the *Zawlbuk* institution was that no women were allowed to enter the *Zawlbuk*. Women received education from their parents, particularly from their mother. Therefore, family education cannot be excluded as traditional Mizo women received education mainly from their home. As Chatterji rightly says

> As formal education and teaching had not yet established itself as a super temporal method, the family was still then an instrument for the educating the newcomers in the society. But the weakness and inadequacies of such a measure to meet the real needs of the society were counteracted through the collective mechanism of the *Zawlbuk*.[42]

To some extent, *Zawlbuk* can be regarded as an expansion of family education to meet the social requirements. However, from the feminist perspective, as women were not allowed to enter in the *Zawlbuk* where important things were discussed, it is evidence that women did not interfere in the important meetings concerning the social welfare. They were voiceless in the society and most of the decision-making was done without the presence of women, unless their chief was a woman.

Mizo Women and Education

As mentioned earlier, *Zawlbuk* education was limited to the young men of the village. Hence, the educational function of the family, the role of a mother cannot be excluded in its educational functions of the traditional Mizo society. R.S Pandey rightly said, family is the most important agency of education before the establishments of school and parents were responsible for the education of their children.[43] The noteworthiness and uniqueness of the family in traditional Mizo society were that there was no other place for the women to receive education, whereas, the men have had. Most of the household works were done by women. John Shakespeare comments on the hard work of the women of the Mizos saying:

> Having conveyed her basketful to the house, she has to set to work cleaning the rice for the day. The necessary amount of rice has been dried the previous day on the shelf over the hearth, and this she now proceeds to pound in a mortar in the front verandah, and winnow on an oval bamboo till it is clean enough for use, the breakfast of rice has then to be cooked and by the time it is ready, her husband is awake. After the meal the real work of the day begins.[44]

The mother's role in the traditional educational system was to prepare her daughters to be great spouse and proficient in weeding and harvesting. She had to play the role of a caregiver and instructor to each of her children. She had to illustrate this reality by way of setting model through hard work and her lifestyle. Consequently, from the age of 6 or 7, a mother had to teach her daughter to collect firewood for the family, to carry drinking water, and to look after the younger brothers or sisters. In addition to these skills, a mother had to train her daughter so that, as soon as she attained puberty, she would be competent of joining others in sowing, weeding, and harvesting. Another teaching session for a mother was at bedtime when mothers told stories to their children. Through listening to these tales, children took on new learning experiences. Basic information about Mizo culture and customs was communicated to children in this manner.

Within the family, the girl child received education more than the boy child. This does not mean that the boy does not receive education from home. During mealtime, the father, the head of the family, communicated a word of instruction for their children.[45] It is said that the mealtime was the only time in which the family members were together at home. The mealtime was an important session for discussing family matters as well as teaching the children as a whole. C.L. Hminga says: "At mealtime when the whole family would sit in a circle on the floor, eating food from a large common wooden plate, the father would give assignments of work to the family members and would speak words of advice or caution to his children."[46]

> Certainly, the words of the father were crucial for bringing up the moral conduct and ethics of the children. The father organized his own technique, as he considers the best for his children. He was concerned with what may truly make his children valuable and faithful citizens in their grown-up life and how they may well be offer assistant to others for the well-being of the society.[47]

Hence, combination of the particular parts of the father, the mother, and the *Val Upa* were the sources of the traditional education system among the Mizo for the welfare of the village. Mizo children were empowered to develop a solid character and this aspect of teaching was the sole obligation of the father. The educational exercises at home and in the Zawlbuk were intended to have a social value.

2. Contents of the Mizo Traditional Education

During the period of pre-literature and informal education in Mizoram, in fact, there was no systematic syllabus as such in the present-day education. However, the important elements of the contents of the Mizo traditional education can be pointed out.

Moral Value and Civic Sense

Where family or *Zawlbuk* was the educational institution, the central contents of the education focused on the moral and the civic sense of the Mizo, which were to the welfare of the society and to end up with a loyal citizen. One of the significant aspects of the contents of education was no other than what is termed as *Tlawmngaihna*.

Tlawmngaihna

The most significant and remarkable sociocultural value and civic sense imparted among the Mizos was *Tlawmngaihna*. *Tlawmngaihna* is the term used for the ethical value or moral conduct of the Mizo. It is not easy to define *Tlawmngaihna* in short sentences. N.E. Parry who was one of those who knew in depth the life and culture of the Mizos said that "*Tlawmngaihna*" is a term, which has no exact equivalent term in English. It really represents the Mizos' code of moral and good forms.[48] He feels that *Tlawmngaihna* can really only be explained by example. Therefore, he gave different situational examples for proper understanding of *Tlawmngaihna*. Let us point three examples from N.E Parry's writing:

> **Helping the sick**-It is the custom in Lushai villages, if a man is sick, for all the villagers to combine and carry him into the hospital. Supposing some one from a far away village has to be carried into hospital, he is carried by his own villagers to the next village and thence by the inhabitants of that village to the next and so on until the hospital is reach. When any one has to be carried in this way, two young man who are known as Zualko (means messenger) are sent to the next village to inform the villagers that a sick man is on the way. A soon as they get the news the villagers abandon whatever they are doing and go to meet the sick man. A village that possesses Thlawmngaihna will go to meet the convoy at the boundary of their lands and offer to carry the sick man from there. If the villagers who are already carrying are also keen on Tlawmngaihna they will refuse to hand over their burden and will insist on carrying it right up to the village. A village that does this is showing the right spirit and actually practising Tlawmngaihna.[49]

> If a man falls sick in the cultivating season, his fellow villagers are expected to weed his field for him. The Chief will probably call for volunteers for this work and if the rules of *Tlawmngaihna* are properly followed in the village there will be numerous volunteers to do the work.[50]

> According to the custom all travelers in the hills are entitled to food and lodging free for night. Some people churlishly refuse to give

the hospitality required by custom but one who follow the rules of *Tlawmngaihna* will never refuse hospitality to stranger and the more strangers a man puts the more *Tlawmngaihna* he is held to possess.[51]

J.H. Lorrain, one of the pioneer missionaries to Mizoram, also had given seven points to define *Tlawmngaihna*. The points given by Lorrain in his dictionary are—(1) to be self-sacrificing, unselfish, self-denying, persevering, stoical, stout-hearted, plucky, brave, firm, independent, loath to lose one's reputation, prestige, too proud or self-respecting to give in, etc. (2) To persevere, to endure patiently, to make light of personal injuries, to dislike making a fuss about anything. (3) To put one's own inclinations on one side and do a thing that one would rather not do, with the object either of keeping up one's prestige, etc. or of helping or pleasing another, etc. (4) To do whatever occasion demand no matter how distasteful or inconvenient it may be to oneself or to one's own inclinations. (5) To refuse to give in, give way, or be conquered. (6) To not like to refuse a request; to do a thing because one does not like to refuse or because one wishes to please others and (7) to act pluckily or show a brave front.[52] This shows the limitation of English words and phrases to explain or define *Tlawmngaihna*. H.L. Malsawma also says "*Tlawmngaihna* cannot be easily explained in theory; it is a practical Mizo life character."[53]

Tlawmngaihna, thus can mean a morale or ethic that urges a person to perform good things for others, without expecting a return. It is an emotional as well as rational response, which persists a person to volunteer himself/herself for others according to their needs. *Tlawmngaihna* is against selfishness, self-praise, and immoral and unethical actions and it is for the welfare of the people.

Zawlbuk and *Tlawmngaihna* are deeply connected to each other. As Mangkhosat Kipgen said, the most important outcome of *Zawlbuk* training with lasting effect was the development and perfection of *Tlawmgngaihna*.[54] In the *Zawlbuk*, the young Mizo were taught, molded, and encouraged by the elders to be a *Tlawmngai* person, which was practically done for the welfare of the society. It could be said that the *Tlawmngaihna* bounded the whole community of the traditional Mizo society.

In general, the significances of *Tlawmngaihna* can be listed as:

- *Tlawmngaihna* ensures peace and security in the village

The primitive Mizo society so often formed confederacy with other villages of the same tribe for pursuing war against foes. Apart from headhunting and intervillage war, the village life was occasionally imperiled by the constant attack of savage wild animals upon their domestic animals and human being as well. The security and peace of the village were the essential concern in the primitive Mizo society. The security and peace of the village could be well maintained because of the *Tlawmngai* people. *Tlawmngaihna* could be considered the fundamental principle that played the role in keeping up the peace and security of the village.[55]

- *Tlawmngaihna* is the basic factor of voluntary service

The Mizo village life depended on the voluntary social service of the villagers. There were times when the villagers ought to contribute their service for the welfare of the village like—when there is need to make footpaths between villages or between the cultivated land, construction of the widows' house, etc. Each member was in need of another in different situations or particular crisis. The voluntary service could be performed only because of *Tlawmngaihna*.[56] They lean on each other for the well-being of society.

- *Tlawmngaihna* is the basic factor of sharing with other

The imperative characteristic of the Mizo culture like sharing belongings, delight, and joy could only be practiced because of the outcome of *Tlawmngaihna. Tlawmngaihna* might be seen as the fundamental factor of sharing with others both in joyful times as well as in the event of distress.

- *Tlawmngaihna* maintained personal discipline

Tlawmngaihna not only maintained the community welfare but also kept up personal discipline. In Mizo history, we see heroes like *Vanapa, Taitesena, Chawngbawla*, etc., who were famous and remembered for their *Tlawmngaihna* and they are the models and glory of *Tlawmngaihna*. The *Tlawmngai* (verb form) persons are exceedingly esteemed, respected, and regarded within the village. To be a *Tlawmngai* person, a person needed to discipline himself/herself. Therefore, the vital force of *Tlawmngaihna* maintained personal discipline.

Therefore, the value of *Tlawmngaihna* in the traditional Mizo society cannot be overemphasized. The entire institution of the Mizo community was bounded by *Tlawmngaihna*. The central or the core principle of the Mizo traditional education was *Tlawmngaihna*.

Arts and Crafts

Arts and crafts can be claimed as one of the contents of the Mizo traditional education. In the primitive culture of the Mizo society, they were a migratory people. Therefore, they hardly possessed a large quantity of household materials. However, the Mizo handwork was seemed to be so excellent. Mac Call also made a meaningful comment saying,

> ...in the face of such unpromising conditions it is all the more surprising that the quality of Lushai handwork attained it's recognized excellent. However, they never made for commercial purpose. The indigenous arts like weaving, basket making, pottery, metal working, lacquering, and blacksmithing were falls under the demand of each family.[57]

Thus, it was only to meet their own needs where they mainly applied their skill. Weaving was one of the significant craft skills in the traditional Mizo culture. The full process of weaving takes time, therefore, it requires patience and time. The cotton collected from the forest is ginned to eliminate its seed by means of a locally made ginning machine. The cotton is then softened by means of a cane string of a bow, then the soft cotton is sprung by hand, and the cotton finally runs into a length of threads. About the weaving work of Mizo women, Mac Call remarks, "The weaving is excellent, and is done on complicated indigenous handlooms, home grown cotton being used. The whole process requires patience and time."[58] Young ladies began to learn the art of weaving from their mother or elder sister, beginning with a small loom, known as *Themlem*. With practice, the girl learned cotton weaving. This was carried out broadly by the ladies. In fact, weaving was an obligatory household work for women.[59]

Household baskets were all made of plaited bamboo, usually by the menfolk and were fortified by hefty cane, which was exceptionally hard and durable. It was colored and a pattern was created burning (smoking) the cane. Baskets were used for preserving valuables in the house, carrying woods for ladies, carrying rice, etc.[60] Every mature menfolk was required to make a basket by himself and it was the responsibility of the father to teach his son.

Other than these weaving and basket making, potteries and metal working were also essential necessities in the traditional

Mizo society. The blacksmith also occupied an important place in the Mizo society. The skills of arts and crafts were imparted practically by the parents and older friends in the villages.

Religious Values

Most writers portray the Mizo religion as animism. A.G. McCall had said "Before the British occupied their land, the Lushai (Mizo) were wholly animism."[61] The missionaries to Mizoram in 1920s, E. Chapman and M.Clark also said that "When we arrived in 1919 there were few Christians. The people were animists; they believe in spirits, and thought that every tree, hill and stone was inhabited by spirit."[62] One of the Mizo historians, Rev. Liangkhaia, opines that the religion of the Mizos had its origin within the perception of their requirement for deliverance from physical sickness and from other uneven circumstances that they attribute to the malevolent spirit.[63] They made a sacrifice to malevolent spirit due to their fear of illness and misfortune; hence, the sacrifices were done by a village priest.[64] However, they did not worship the malevolent spirit rather they believed in the existence of a benevolent spirit or supreme Spirit. For fear of displeasing the malevolent spirit, the priest gave sacrifices to the malevolent spirit in order to please the malevolent spirit.

The Mizo Understanding of Life after Death

The Mizo believed in life after death. The spirit world is believed to be two places, separated by a river called *Pial*. One place is called *Pialral* (a place beyond the river of Pial) where life is extravagant, plenty to eat and no need to work. Only those who earned the title *Thangchhuah* can enter the *Pialral*. The other place is called *Mitthi khua* meaning village of the dead, where life is dull and colorless.[65] Therefore, in religious aspect, a Mizo's highest value was to earn the title of *Thangchhuah*.

Hence, the title of *Thangchhuah* was regarded as a permit to *Pialral* or heaven.[66]

There were two ways how to earn the title of *Thangchhuah*:

1. *Home Thangchhuah:* which one was able to attain on the basis of wealth possessed by the villager known as *In lama Thangchhuah*. Home *Thangchhuah* could be earned by giving a certain number of open feasts.

2. Outdoor *Thangchhuah:* This was known as *Ram lama Thangchhuah*. In order to achieve outdoor *Thangchhuah*, a person had to be an imminent hunter, He must kill a number of prescribed wild animals such as bear, deer, wild gayal, sambar deer, wild bear, *Rulngan* (a huge poisonous snake), hawk.[67]

Hence, to perform outdoor *Thangchhuah,* one must be courageous, heroic and he must be well known or a notable hunter as he was required to kill a number of wild animals. Home *Thangchhuah* was performed by a wealthy man who conducted a series of ceremonial feasts and penances. Subsequently, to perform home *Thangchhuah,* one man must become a rich person and only few people could get the title in this kind of *Thangchhuah*.

The wife of *Thangchhuah* man also enjoyed her husband's title, and the wife along with the children were permitted to wear a special cloth name *Thangchhuah Puan (Thangchuah Cloth).*[68]

J.V. Hluna says "*Thangchhuah* was the most coveted goal which every Mizo longed to perform, and thereby their whole endeavour [sic] throughout life centred [sic] in trying to achieve this goal."[69] Thus, in religious aspect, one of the foremost esteem in Mizo traditional society was *Thangchhuah*. In traditional Mizo society, the one who got the title of *Thangchhuah* was respected and honored in the villages. Therefore, every Mizo gave much effort to get *Thangchhuah* title.

Mizos have their own cultural values that are included in the contents of informal education. Besides the above mentioned contents, Mizo traditional education included sports activities and other religious ceremonies. All these cultural values are imparted among the Mizo by different methods and means of education.

3. The Method and Means of Imparting Value System

All the sociocultural values that have been discussed were imparted among the Mizo from generation to generation. As mentioned before, in spite of the fact that there was no formal education, the Mizos maintained their own ways and methods to promote the sociocultural values. Let us examine how the sociocultural value was imparted among the Mizos.

Setting a Reward

In every village, there was a title set aside for *Tlawmngai* person called *"Tlawmngai Nopui dawm thei."* In English translation, it goes like this "Who is capable of holding a cup of *Tlawmngaihna."* Every youth in the village put a serious effort to get this title. A cup of rice beer was offered in the event of social gathering. The cup of rice beer did not matter most, but the acknowledgment of one as *"tlawmngai nopui dawmthei"* (the title) was extremely difficult to attain and it was exceedingly respectful.[70] The chief encouraged the villagers to be a *Tlawmngai* person by giving adoration and motivation.

One incident may be pointed out to illustrate how the chief encouraged the young men: Once a Chief Hrangvunga of Serhmun village tried to find out the most *tlawmngai* person among his villagers. One stormy night, the Chief sent his elder to the *Zawlbuk* to inquire for a volunteer to travel to another village which was situated on the other side of the river, and convey an urgent message to his brother. No one was willing to go out so late at night and in such weather as there were many dangers on the way. But a young brave man called Taitesena promptly arrived at the chief's house and was ready to go. To his surprise, when he arrived at the chief's house, the chief informed him of the real reason and welcomed him to a drink honoring his courage. The following day, the chief informed the whole village through the village Crier proclaiming Taitesena as "the most loyal to the chief as well as the outstanding *Tlawmngai* person among the three hundred young men of the villagers." This is one of the strategies of how the chief imparted the value of *Tlawmngaihna* among his people by encouraging, appreciating, and giving high regard to them.[71]

However, there was no such title for the women in the Mizo society. On the other hand, while giving due recognition to the qualities of *Tlawmngaihna*, it was a remarkable thing that the equally high qualities of *Tlawmngaihna* were found among the girls. It is unfortunate that many writers failed to recognize the quality of Tlawmngaihna among the girls. Respected Challiana, a first-generation pastor of the BCM who was baffled commented that it was astonishing to find out how the Mizo girls remained healthy and strong doing numerous physical work in comparison to the little amount of food they consumed and little sleep they got.

As describe by Challiana on the hard work of Mizo girls which is translated in English by Mangkhosat Kipgen is worthy to quote here-

> At seven or eight years old, when the girls can carry two bamboo-water tubes on her back, the mother will begin teaching her the ways of Tlawmngaihna. She would teach her how to

carry water, collect firewood, husk paddy, and winnowing it, cook the family food, feed the pigs, and entice the fowls to the coop. Besides, while the parents work in the jhum, she would look after the baby, if there was one and thus would be busy the whole day. When she becomes a maiden, she would learn weaving, continuing the entire household work, and also start joining her parents in the jhum work. When the night comes, the young men of the village would go around to court girls in their home. Although they may be tired, a Tlawmngai girl would welcome them warmly. While chitchatting with the young men, she would still be busy with cooking food for pigs, spinning cotton, rolling the thread into ball, or mending torn cloths. When the young men were ready to leave, she should extend to make them feel that they are much welcome to stay on and they usually farewell with open words saying that please do come again in other night. Therefore, girls of the traditional Mizo society practically had no time to rest."[72]

When the missionaries came into Mizoram, they had observed the hard work of the Mizo women. Dorothy Grovers says:

> Every house hold work has been done by the women. Mizo women were busy house keepers and workers. Besides the care of the children and cooking, she was a spinner, weaver, dressmaker, water-carrier, wood—cutter. She also looked after the domestic animals and helped with the cultivation.[73]

Rokhuma also rightly made a comment when he says "Women also maintained the spirit of *Tlawmngaihna.*"[74] One of the worst features of traditional Mizo society was the position of women. In spite of hard work in the family, they were voiceless and had no right to inheritance.

Folktales

One of the ways in which the custom and social value of the Mizo was transmitted from one generation to the next generation was through storytelling. A few stories were told by the mother to their children at bedtime, but it was in the *Zawlbuk,* where the most important storytelling was done.[75] Mangkhosat Kipgen classified the Mizo folktale into three types as: legend, jokes, and patriotic stories. It is not possible to discuss all the folk stories, therefore; focus will be given to patriotic stories as it played a significant role in motivating *Tlawmngaihna* to the young men.

The Patriotic Stories

The patriotic stories included stories of a long list of extraordinary and courageous men of the past, by which the young men were encouraged to be a *Tlawmngai* person. The Mizos had numerous stories concerning heroes. These storytelling were intended to inspire the listener to follow the footsteps of the heroes known as *Pasaltha*.[76] The more popular heroes of the Mizos were Khuangchera of Reiek village, Jampuimanga of Jampui village, Chawngbawla of Seipui village, Saizahawla of Khawruhlian, Taitesena, Vanapa, etc.[77] All these stories of heroes were narrated by the parents to their children at home and by the elders to the young men within the *Zawlbuk*.

Mac Call and Parry hold the same supposition that the predominant purposes of the heroes' stories narrated by the Mizos were to promote *Tlawmngaihna*. The patriotic stories brought out the conception of *Tlawmngaihna,* that it encouraged the Mizos to be courteous, unselfish, courageous, industrious, ready to help others, even at considerable inconvenience to himself, and that he must try to surpass others in doing his ordinary daily tasks efficiently.[78] The enthusiastic patriotic stories, in this manner, altogether significantly played a role in imparting the ethical values within the mindsets of the Mizos.

Mizo Sayings/Proverbs

In order to maintain a moral well-being, Mizos also had a number of proverbs and sayings in educating the people. One of the goals of education was to teach sound ethical behavior.

This was instilled by several maxims. Some of the Mizo maxims translated in English are cited from *Chawngthanpari*.[79]

Relation to Moral Character

In emphasizing the importance of personal character: the Mizo maxim was, "*Nun chhiat leh suahsual a siam theih a, hmelchhiat a siam that theih loh*," which means "bad habits and misconduct can be set right, but an ugly face cannot be changed." This maxim was to encourage people to be able to change bad character. In fact, an ugly person cannot change his or her face, however, he or she can change the bad propensities' misconduct.

In respect to kindness to creation, the guidelines go, "*Rannung pawi sawi lo sawi sak leh an chunga nun rawn hi vanduaina thlentu leh thihna rapthlak thentu ani*," which means "it is not right to abuse harmless creatures and animals. If one indulges in such ill treatment, he will incur miserable suffering and a terrible death."

From a moral point of view, stealing was condemned and considered as a serious offense against the society, hence it was directly expressed, "It is illegal to steal."[80] They believed that once someone stole something, he or she must face an untimely death. For instance, stealing a hoe or a spade, which were used for digging grave, would lead to the use of the same instrument to dig the grave of the one who stole it. In short, it means that the thief will not live long.

Parents have a maxim for their children, "Those who do not care for their parents will not prosper." And with the purpose of teaching, the importance of controlling the tongue, "A person with a careless tongue will not live long."[81]

In teaching humility and guarding against pride, "*Mahni infak leh sakhi ngalah engmah a bet lo*," meaning, "just as there is no flesh on the leg of a deer, there is no worth in self-praise."

Relation to Personal Relationship

In relation to personal relationship: some sayings were:

"*Sem sem dam dam, Ei bil thi thi.*" The literal translation goes like this "who share belonging must live and who eat alone must die." This implies that the moral of generosity must be followed and one must care for others.

"*Lampui Changkhatah mi an be chhe ngai lo*" which means "never speak rudely to anyone you may meet on the road."

"*Tawngkam thain sial a man*," which means speaking kind words worth a huge prize (*Sial*).[82]

"*Anchhe lawh hi mahni chungah a tla thin*," literally means "cursing others will fall on the curser," which implies that one must be careful not to harm or imprecate others.

"*Lungpui pawh lungtein a kamki loh chuan a awm thei lo*," literally means "a huge stone could not stand alone without leaning against a small stone." It implies that everyone is important to each other, even a powerful person lean against the weak person.

Relation to the Neighborhood

In relation to the neighborhood, some sayings are:

"*Khaw sarih do aiin thenawmte do a hrehawm zawk*" which literally means a conflict with neighbors is more unpleasant than having a war with seven villages. This implies the values of having a close relationship with the people staying close to each other.

"*Ri te hriat loha ramri zauh chu thihna a ni,*" which simply means extending the boundary of land or cultivated area without the knowledge of the neighbor would bring death.

These sayings reflected the moral obligation of one's duty to maintain a good relationship with their neighbors.

Relation to Superstition

In relation to superstition, some of the sayings are:

"Kawnah Ram huai a liam duh," which means that the saddle of the hill is haunted by malevolent spirit. Therefore, for the Mizos in their traditional society, such place was not suitable to construct a house, rather it was a fearful place for them.

"*Lungpui leh thing lianin Huai an nei*" which literally means that a large tree and a huge stone commonly possessed malevolent spirit.

"*Khawkang leh Sakei sehah awm ni kham tur a ni*" which means that whenever there was a fire in the village, and if a person died from a tiger attack, no one must work in their cultivated land.

Other than these sayings, there are several maxims in relation to taboo, which the Mizos strictly followed throughout a long part of their history, all of which cannot be listed here.

Relation to Women

According to Chatterji, "In Mizo society, women were not treated equally with men; they were placed at a very insignificant position. In spite of this, they were treated with love and care, and adorned in much the same manner as men were treated."[83] However, it is also opined strongly by certain sections of people that women were put down to the lowest status of social hierarchical order though they played a significant role within the family in particular and in the sociopolitical life of the Mizos in general.

Certain people cited some derogatory sayings in order to exhibit the low status of women in primitive Mizo society. Some sayings are: "*Hmeichia leh palchhia chu a thlak leh theih zel*" which literally means "women (wives) and fences can be effortlessly supplanted." Women were compared with bamboo fences of their small domestic vegetable farms that needs to be replaced when it becomes old.

Another saying is "*Hmechhe finin tuikhur ral a kai lo*" which literally means "The wisdom of a woman does not extend beyond the limit of the village water source." This indicates that women were not wise enough to make a decision. Other saying goes like this "A woman is like a walnut tree, the more you beat them the better they become." Another saying states that "Even as crab's meat is no meat, a woman's words are no words." Thus, from some of these sayings, the position of women in Mizo traditional society is clearly portrayed.

Most of the sayings functioned as the guiding principles of the Mizo moral conduct. It was handed over from generation to generation. It helped them to live a disciplined life and develop character traits consonant with the virtues that accorded with their social norms. Such principles provided ethical and moral teachings for harmonious social relationships. On the contrary, if one failed to follow such principles, he or she could be looked down upon by the society. Therefore, almost all the proverbial saying focuses to inculcate moral value to the Mizos' mind. However, to some extent, some of the sayings particularly with regard to the Mizo women could be also treated as immoral.

Educational Value of Folk Song

Singing and dancing are related to each other in a traditional Mizo society. The Mizos are singing tribes, they have passion for singing and dancing. According to H.L. Malsawma, "Their poetry portrays their emotion and thought in extreme simplicity. Whether in war or peace the Mizo must sing the event."[84] Mizos expressed their joys and sorrows by singing and dancing. It is the integral part of the Mizo society. B. Lalthangliana Mizo, a historian, pointed out some of the dances of the Mizos, which have steps particularly in their way of dance, like—*Khual lam; Cheraw; Chai; Solakia; Rallulam;* etc.[85] Mizos have a variety of cultural dances that have their own steps.

Singing and dancing are some of the cultural values of the Mizo community. This is deeply rooted in Mizo society. Lalrinawmi Ralte rightly observes "Song, drum, and dance make up a powerful union because they share their common roots in the life of the Mizo. Together, song, drum, and dances expressed the deep spirituality of the Mizo."[86] Song, singing, and dancing played a significant role in the Mizo society. Mizos share their joy and sorrow through singing songs and dancing. In joyful occasion like festivals, there were no other means than singing and dancing to express their joy and happiness. Likewise when there was a sad or sorrowful occasion, the villagers gathered together and started singing in the bereaved family's house. They shared and comforted their sorrow by singing.

Conclusion

Before the arrival of the western missionaries, the Mizos did not have formal education. They did not even have a written script. The traditional Mizo society was well set up under the administration of the chief. The home and *Zawlbuk* were the only institutions where the Mizos received education to meet the needs of their society, family as well as individual. One of the limitations of the *Zawlbuk* institution was that it excluded women education. Some of the Mizo sayings in relation to the women reflected the low status of women in traditional Mizo society.

In such a context of the Mizo society, *Tlawmngaihna* was one of the core values of the traditional education of the Mizo, which could be considered the core principle of the moral conduct of the Mizos. The central focus of the Mizo traditional education was *Tlawmngaihna*. Folk stories especially patriotic stories and Mizo proverbial sayings played an important role in imparting the moral code of conduct and civic sense in traditional Mizo society. They became an important means for educating the Mizos.

Therefore, before the arrival or the advent of the British colonial power, the Mizos had their own way of education and sociocultural values. They were isolated from other cultures and were self-sufficient in terms of economy and village administration. It was in this context that the western missionaries entered Mizoram and preached the Gospel and established formal education system. The British colonial power and the Christian Mission played a significant role in the rapid change of the Mizo society in terms of its socioreligious culture, which will be discussed in the next chapter.

Chapter 2

The Beginning and Development of Mission School Education in Mizoram

As it has been discussed in the previous chapter, during the early part of the 18th century, Mizoram was an unexplored and almost unknown land to most of the world even after the British had occupied Northeast India. The advent of the British in Mizoram played an important factor in the beginning of a new era for the Mizos. After the exploration of Mizoram by the British, Arthington's Mission entered Mizoram in 1894. A mission school was started in the same year. The British Government of Assam turned over all aspects of education in Mizoram to the missionaries in 1904, both in the northern and southern parts of Mizoram. Then after India became independent in 1952, the responsibility was given back to the Government.

In this chapter, this process of transformation and change from the traditional to the modern educational system will be analyzed; first, the beginning of the British administration in Mizoram will be dealt with as it played an important role in the coming of the missionaries to Mizoram and second, how the mission schools began, the system of education, and the content and curriculum of the same will be analyzed. Third, whether there was inconsistency or obstacle, in the process of transition from traditional education to formal education will be looked at.

1. The British in Mizoram

Until the later part of the 19th century, the British Indian Government did not interfere in the affairs of the Lushai hills. On many occasions, the Mizos murdered tea-garden native workers in Cachar and elsewhere, carrying off the heads of the victims as trophies. In the course of those raids, Chittagong, Sylhlet, Cachar, Manipur, and Tripura became frequent targets of the Mizos. Almost two decades prior to 1854, the Mizos had raided the neighboring plains 19 times.[87]

There could be many factors for the frequent raids on the neighboring people by the Mizo. J.V. Hluna states some of the reasons:[8]: First, the Mizos were proud of their adventures. For them, raids were equivalent to wars. The status and position of the chiefs were illustrious based on the number of successful attacks they made. Second, the Mizos adapted using gun and gunpowder since 1824–1826. Gun and gun power became a passion for the chiefs as they knew the plain people had these. Third, it was also for obtaining articles like bell-metal plates, bangles, and other materials, which they considered valuable, which were available in the plains. They also sought salt and other foodstuffs, which was another reason for the frequent raids by the Mizos on the neighboring tribes and plains people.

Hluna further gives a remark that raids became more frequent only after the advent of the British rule in Cachar and the neighboring areas. In the early period, there were no interventions by other rulers of the neighboring states to the Mizo hills. The frequent raids on the British were mostly in the form of a protest against colonial intervention.[89] Rev. Zairema also states that the reason for the Mizos attacking the Alexandrapur Tea Garden was mainly to protecting their claimed land area which was occupied by the tea plantation. For the tribal people, land is the main source of their livelihood. They might not occupy the land in the area of Alexandrapur, still then it was their hunting area, Zairema said.[90]

Therefore, it is not strange and unreasonable for the Mizos to raid their neighboring land. The Mizo chiefs were alert in trying to protect their land from their neighboring tribes. As a result of frequent raids by the Mizos on its neighboring people, the first British official expedition against the Lushai was launched in 1871. One of the immediate reasons for sending such a military expedition was the murder of James Winchester, a tea-planter. The Mizos carried off his 6-year-old daughter Mary as their captive.[91] The military expedition to rescue Mary Winchester began to open up the Mizo Hills to the British. Consequently, villages were burnt and chiefs held responsibly were fined and punished. After the military expedition, there was a peace agreement between the Mizos and the British in 1871.[92]

One of their agreements was that the plain people must be permitted to enter Mizoram with a submission of tax to the British Government of India. Accordingly, a number of plain people entered Mizoram and made settlements doing their trade and business. There was peace for about 16 years. However, as the population of the plain people entering Mizoram rapidly increased, again the Mizos continued raids on the plain businessmen at *Changsil* village and other places. In one way, it can be said that the Mizos were trying to defend themselves from the assimilation of other cultures.[93]

The second expedition was launched in 1889–1890. One of the immediate reasons for the second expedition was that the two brothers of the Mizo Chief Lianphunga and Zahrawka sons of Suakpuilala raided the Chengri plain near Rangamati, Chittagong. They burned 24 villages killing 101 people and 91 people were taken as captives.[94] This incident resulted in the second military expedition against the Lushais. It was much greater than the first expedition. It was found that a few years prior to the final Lushai Expedition (1889–1890), the Mizos conducted 17 raids into British territory with varying intensities and results. Such raids into the plains gave rise to massive British punitive expeditions into the hills. The British Indian Government decided to govern the Lushai Hills.[95]

In 1890, the British divided Mizoram into two administrative centers, the Southern and the Northern Parts, Lunglei and Aizawl became the centers of administration, respectively.[96] Major John Shakespeare was the first superintendent stationed at Aizawl as a representative of the Viceroy of India.[97] These changes under the British marked the end of a long period of isolation for the Mizos and an end to warfare and raids. Most of the Mizo chiefs were subdued by1893.[98]

Meanwhile, the pioneer missionaries J.H. Lorrain and F.W Savidge were waiting for permission from the British Government official to enter Mizoram. Due to the disturbed area of Mizoram, J.H. Lorrain and F.W. Savidge were not allowed to enter Mizoram by the British officials.

The two missionaries stayed at Silchar for more than 1 year waiting for the permission of the Government. In 1893, while staying at Silchar, through the Deputy Commissioner of Silchar, they wrote an application to the superintendent of Mizoram to grant permission to them for entering Mizoram.

But the reply was that they had to wait for another year and they would be allowed to enter the hill only after the area became more peaceful. Then in the month of December 1893, Sir Ward, Deputy Commissioner of Silchar, had a conversation with J.H. Lorrain and after he promised that they would not interfere in the British administration and not oppose the British administration in Mizoram, they were finally allowed to enter the Hill.[99] This evidenced that British administrative officials were deeply involved in the life of the missionaries in entering Mizoram.

Later when the British occupied Mizoram with their military power and administrative system, the missionaries were enabled to spread the Christian faith among the Mizos. Thus, Mizoram, and the people, which were unexplored and isolated from the outside world came to be known by the mission agencies. Therefore, the British colonial power played an important role in the coming of the missionaries to Mizoram.

2. The Beginning of Mission School Education in Mizoram

The first pioneer missionaries J. Herbert Lorrain and F.W. Savidge, members of High Gate Baptist Church in London, came to Mizoram under the Arthington Mission and worked there for 4 years. After working for almost 4 years in Mizoram, Lorrain and Savidge had to leave Mizoram on the instruction of the Mission Board that sponsored them. Robert Arthington, the founder of the Mission, urged them to turn to other unreached regions by the Gospel. He had a strong prejudice against the institutionalization of mission work. His primary objective was the proclamation of the Gospel where it was not preached. He opined that as soon as a small Christian fellowship should come up, missionaries should press on to regions as yet unreached.[100] After they left, Foreign Mission of the Presbyterian

Church of Wales sent D.E Jones, who reached Aizawl on August 1987.[101] D.E Jones continued the work of Lorrain and Savidge.

The general assembly of the Presbyterian Church of Wales 1902 agreed to transfer the southern part of Mizoram to the BMS in London. J.H Lorrain and F.W. Savidge who left Mizoram at the end of 1897 returned to Mizoram in 1903 as missionaries of the BMS in London.[102] In 1903, in terms of the mission field, Mizoram was divided between the Presbyterians, who took care of the northern part and the Baptist Mission, who took care of the southern part, to which Lorrain and Savidge came back to the southern part of Mizoram in 1903.[103]

3. The Transition of the Traditional System of Education

The following discussion deals with how and why the Mizo traditional system of education was replaced by the mission school education.

Oral Form into the Written Form of Education

The means of instruction in Mizo traditional system of education was oral form of education. The oral system of education was transformed by the missionaries to a written form of education. Why did the missionaries place such an emphasis upon creating a written language?

Frederick Downs had a simple answer to this question saying that in the first place, education was central to their evangelistic method and they were committed to educate the Mizos in their mother tongue. One of the characteristic emphases of the protestant missions from its beginnings in the 16th century had been also the use of mother tongue in both worship and the reading of the Bible.[104] This emphasis on the importance of the native language came to be reinforced by the democratic ideologies of French and American revolutions in the idea of many evangelicals who came from "non-conformist and American Baptist missionaries."[105] They, therefore, supported giving education in the mother tongue rather than in a superior tongue. As Downs says, "a written language is necessary for education, and the best education would be given in a people's own language."[10]

A second reason for the necessity of making people literate was that they could read the Bible. From the evangelical viewpoint, the Christian lifestyle and the spiritual sustenance required the ability to read the scripture. They could not conceive a healthy and self-sufficient Christianity without the availability of the Bible in their own language.[107] Therefore, the primary purpose of creating a written language and using the mother tongue as a medium of instruction was to provide materials for use in schools and translating scriptures in the mother tongue for the people. This perception demanded the formulation of alphabets for the Mizos as they did not have any alphabet.

The formulation of Mizo Alphabet

It is necessary to underline how the Mizo alphabet came into being. It is interesting to note that the two pioneer missionaries began formulating the Mizo alphabets even before they reached Mizoram. Some of the writers like Lalhmuaka and B. Lalthangliana opine that the alphabet of Mizo was probably formulated in the year 1894 after the missionaries arrived at Aizawl.[108] However, though the final form must have been after they arrived in Mizoram, but it is more likely that before entering Mizoram, the alphabet was formulated in the year 1893. As Lloyd says, "It was fortunate that one of the first achievements of Lorrain and Savidge was to invent an alphabet which was highly suitable. No doubt they had been working on this even during the time when they were waiting for permission to enter

Mizoram (1893). At all this events they seem to have been testing the alphabet to see how suitable it was before the end of 1894."[109] For this purpose, they had chosen the simple Roman script, with a phonetic form of spelling based on the well-known Hunterian system.[110] Initially, the arrangement of the alphabet read, A Â B D E F G H I J K L M N O P R S T Ṭ U V Z CH (small letters: a â b d e f g h i j k l m n o p r s t ṭ u v z ch).[111] This alphabet was slightly amended and adopted with mutual agreement between the Welsh missionary educators in the north and the BMS missionaries in the south. The modified form followed, A Â Aw Âw B Ch D E Ê F G H I J K L M N O P R S T Ṭ U Û V Z (small letters: a â aw âw b ch d e ê f g h i j k l m n o p r s t ṭ u û v z.).[112] Later on, they further amended it and finally the present alphabet which has been in use as follows—capital letters: A Aw B Ch D E Ê F G NG H I J K L M N O P R S T Ṭ U V Z (small letters: a aw b ch d e f g ng h i j k l m n o p r s t ṭ u û v z).[113]

With their hard work and determination, the missionaries reduced the Mizo language into written form. It was an incredible achievement for the missionaries to have accomplished the creation of this alphabet and to have opened a school within such a short time. Thus, the missionaries formulated the alphabet of the Mizo on their own and it was neither by the pressure of the native people nor their demand to use the native language as a School medium of instruction. The pioneering missionaries deserve to get credit for reducing the oral language to written form. However, one also needs to critically reevaluate this aspect. Rinchamliana is right when he says:

> The European notion of having the written form of language as the norm was kept at the forefront. However, what the European missionaries failed to realize is that the orality of the Mizo language, where the oral dimension of the language was far more important than having the script. The Europeans pride themselves of reducing

> the Mizo language into a written form without realizing the
> complexity of the Mizo language and putting a language in a written
> form was not the end in itself....it clearly indicated the ignorance
> of the Europeans and their attitude towards language was in terms
> of the Europeans where written form occupies the zenith, on the
> while for a Mizo the oral aspect becomes more important where
> even a single word could mean many things depending on the tones
> and sounds of the word.[114]

To date, there is no consensus even among the educated people and Mizo writers in the correct writing of the Mizo language. For instance, concerning the punctuation of whether the words are to be joined or not to be joined, it seems that the missionaries gave no proper emphasis on the correct way of writing. Rather they were more concerned with putting the language into writing. For example, whether to join the prefix and suffix in a word, and also adding of "v" as in *silova* or *siloa*, adding of "v" on such kinds of words seems to be the product of the pioneer foreign missionaries, which till today, such kinds of problems have not yet been rectified. Moreover, the oral form stands more meaningful in Mizo language. As Lloyd rightly observes saying "the Mizo language is basically monosyllabic. Each syllable has its own pitch, tone length and special emphasis... words therefore tend to preserve their own form and pattern".[115] According to the tone, the same word can mean different things in Mizo language. For example, the words "*Lei*" can mean human tongue, sand, bridge, buying, slope, etc. B. Lalthangliana also writes "As Mizo language is a tonal language, till today we do not have a proper symbol of the different tone."[116] Therefore, it is a great challenge for educated Mizos to find a consensus way of writing the Mizo language particularly in the joining of certain words.

It is also necessary to acknowledge the two natives, Suaka and Thangphunga, who made a great contribution to the formulation of the Mizo alphabet as well as Bible translation.

Suaka and Thangphunga worked as superintendent's *Rah-si* (circle-interpreter) at the time of the two missionaries Lorrain and Savidge arrived in Mizoram.[117] They worked with the missionaries in collecting the Mizo vocabularies and taught the Mizo language to the missionaries in the process of reducing the oral form into written form.[118]

Suaka and Thangphunga became the first among the Mizo to be able to read and write. They were fast learners and they were able to read and write within a month.[119] B. Lalthangliana is right when he acknowledges that though Suaka and Thangphunga were not highly educated in terms of educational qualification, they were keen and intellectual persons. Their availability in helping the missionaries at the time of their arrival was a great privilege for the Mizos. Both of them were honorable and admirable for their contribution toward the formulation of the Mizo language into a written form.[120]

Furthermore, one cannot ignore the significance of the oral form of Mizo language. For instance, their first converts among the Mizos were Khuma and Khara and they were baptized on July 3, 1899 and the irony was that they were both illiterate. Both of them made a great contribution to converting the Mizos to Christianity.[121]

The spread of the Gospel in Mizoram oral system was much effective during the early period of Christianity. With the oral form of informal education, the Mizo had maintained the welfare of the society till then. Moreover, in the Palestinian context in the first century, it is known that before the written script of the Bible, the first-generation Christians passed on the story of Jesus Christ orally and a number of people followed Christ. Therefore, for the growth of Christianity in Mizoram, oral form of spreading the Gospel cannot be ignored as many evangelists were illiterate.

Medium of Instruction

In contrary to the policy of British administration in India, with regard to the medium of instruction, the missionaries put an effort to use the Mizo language as a medium of instruction rather than Bengali before taking over the charge of the government schools.[122] Besides the formation of Mizo alphabet, Lorrain and Savidge also prepared several valuable books for the students as well as for the new believers. In Mizo language with a new alphabet, they prepared *ZirṬan Bu* (Lushai Primer), *Hla Bu* (hymn book), *Zawhna leh Chhanna Bu* (book of questions and answers).[123] These were used as textbooks in their schools.

One of the common issues faced by the missionaries not only in Lushai hill but also in the other hill areas of Assam where language must be applied for the medium of instruction in the school, Assamese or their own native language.[124] Considering the aspects of the issues of the medium of instruction in the school, in 1864, the Governor General in Council laid down that in the future, instruction ought to be given entirely in English or in the indigenous languages of the hill people written in Roman alphabet.[125] However, as their demand was granted in Garo Hills, Khasi, and Jaintia Hills, Bengali was used in their textbooks, still then their mother tongue was used for beginners.[126] In Mizoram, the resolution made in 1864 posed no problem regarding the medium of instruction. There was no demand for either Bengali or Assamese as the medium of instruction.

Most Mizo writers as well as laypeople give credit to the missionaries in Mizoram for their contribution and commitment toward education. In fact, the missionaries deserve to be appreciated for their contribution and effort to use the Mizo alphabet and also for using it as the medium of instruction for the spread of the Gospel. Glover also gives remark that, having the opinion, the importance of teaching in their own language to take a deep root in the hearts of the people. He expressed his opinion saying, "they might not have been such good Christians, if Bengali language was the medium of their Christian teaching."[127]

When it is said, "*Mizo ṭawng*" (Mizo language), it refers to *Duhlian* dialogue. *Duhlian* actually refers to one of the subtribes in Mizoram, who were referred to by the missionaries as "good" or "high" subtribe who could trace their origin the furthest. It was in this dialect the missionaries translated the Bible to. As Lorrain in his letter to T.H. Lewin in 1899 said, they translated the Bible in *Duhlian* Dialect and suggested that they used *Duhlian* as a medium of instruction, however, when the final copy arrived officially they referred to the language as *Lushai*.[128]

The Duhlian dialect has its own history. Although there can be different views on the origin of using Duhlian language among the hill tribes, let me quote from Vumson Suantak here,

"...Then other Zo people moved from the east and settled down speaking dialects different from each other. The Sailo clan who gradually dominated the chieftainship in the area during the late 1600s drove out a larger section of Thado to Cachar and north Manipur. When Lallula Sailo became Chief sometime in 1700s he demanded that the people under his chiefdom speak the same dialect. He was the most powerful Chief in the area during the 1700s. Thus the Duhlian dialect was born. The name Duhlian originated by the fact that that Chief Lalulla demanded high taxation from his subjects so that the dialect he promoted became the Duhlian dialect, 'the dialect of the big demand..[129]

Again it was in this dialect the school textbook was written and all the literatures during the missionary period were written in this dialect.

It is obvious that the use of Mizo language rather than Bengali as the medium of instruction was far more satisfactory for the Mizos. In this regard, all credit must be given to the missionaries. However, there was uncertainty for the acceptance of the *Duhlian* dialect to represent the whole tribes in Lushai hills (alleged to be the Mizo alphabet), which was introduced as the means of instruction.

It is evident that in the traditional Mizo society, there were different dialects as J.M. Llyod says:

> There were a number of kindred tribes all of which could roughly be described as Mizos. They spoke several distinct dialects of Tibeto-Burmese origin. These have gradually been amalgamated and absorbed into *Duhlian* dialect, the language of the Sailo chiefs. This we now call Mizo.[130]

Thus, it was the dialect of the elites, which was used as a medium of instruction in the school, where all other dialects were never regarded. This could be one of the reasons the *Hmar* tribe of the northern area and the *lai* and *Mara* tribes in the southern part of Mizoram contended *Duhlian* dialect and tried to preserve and develop their language; even they wanted to have Bible in their own dialect.

4. The Development of Mission School Education

Although the main focus in this section is the mission school education, it is necessary to highlight the beginning of government schools in Mizoram and how it was handed over to the missionaries for the development of the mission schools.

Transition of Government Schools to Mission Schools

The Government opened schools only for the children of its employees in 1893 at Aizawl and at Lunglei and Demagiri in 1894.[131] The schools were not for the public, it was established mainly for the children of government employees and were maintained by the contributions given by the military police, accompanied by an annual grant of Rs.100.[132] It was in 1897, a government school for the Mizo boys was established with Kavyatirtha as its schoolmaster.[133] However, the medium of instruction of the schools in Mizoram was Bengali.

Mizo writers opined that the British Government of India did not deeply consider the development of the Mizos particularly in the field of education. J.V. Hluna asserts that the Government did not pay much attention to education, but felt it necessary to educate the people for a proper functioning and maintaining of law and order in their society. Thus, it was almost entirely left to the Christian missionaries. The missionaries who perceived education as their ministry accepted the suggestion of the Government.[134] Chawngthanpari also observes, "It appears that the British Government was not giving an important consideration concerning the indigenous system of education, and wanted to substitute it with a system that would serve their purpose to employ the Mizo in their administration. Thus, under their patronage, only a few students benefited from the educational facilities."[135] Thus, under the British Government, school education for the Mizos did not function properly and did not benefit the Mizos much.

In the meantime, as discussed above, the missionaries entered Mizoram in 1894 and started their mission work. Education became an important instrument for its mission. As written by J. Herbert Kane: "Education has always been an integral part of the missionary movement... teaching held an important place in the public ministry of Christ...and played a large role in the development of the Early Church."[136]

Therefore, in Mizoram, education became the main focus of the missionaries' endeavor. When J.H. Lorrain and S.W Savidge arrived in Mizoram in 1894, there was no Mizo vernacular formal educational system for the Mizos. They started a school for the Mizo children on April 1, 1894, according to Lorrain's report.[137] However, after staying for 4 years in Aizawl, due to their Mission policy, they left Aizawl. Jones took over the work of the educational mission in Aizawl under the Foreign Mission of the Presbyterian Church of Wales.

When Lorrain and Savidge arrived at Lunglei in 1903, they made a settlement at Serkawn and they started the school education in the month of July in the same year.[138] As already mentioned before, a government school was already there before the establishment of a mission school in the southern part of Mizoram. However, the mission schools both in the southern part and northern part of Mizoram were much ahead of the government school in terms of quality. The following table[139] shows the result of the first lower primary school examination held in June 1903, indicating the position of the government school and the mission schools.

Table 1 Result of the first lower primary examination 1903.[140]

School	Number of candidates	Number of passed	Number of failed
Government school	14	6	8
Mission school	13	13	–
Total	27	19	8

The number of schools gradually increased but there was no proper system of inspection to cover both the mission school and the government school. H.W.G Cole, Superintendent of Lushai Hills, observed that the Mizos had a great adaptability and obedience, so it was one of the most suitable fields for educational progress than any other hill tribes on the frontier.[141] In this manner, the government officers acknowledged the mission work in their endeavors for education in Mizoram to give advantages to the people.[142] In 1901, Major Shakespeare, the Superintendent had expressed his anticipation that there will be a time when the Christian Mission would take up the entire administration of the school education in Mizoram from the government.[143] Bamfield Fuller, the Chief Commissioner of Assam, visited Mizoram in February 1904, he was impressed by the mission school. He, therefore, inculcated the superintendent to submit a proposal for handing over the entire education to the missionaries.[144]

Subsequently, after the approval of Shakespeare's proposal, the Chief Commissioner appointed Rev. Edwin Rowlands as the honorary inspector of the Schools in both government and the mission school.[145] Correspondingly, the education of the whole of the southern Lushai hills was also put under the care of Mr. Savidge the same year (1904).[146] Thus, all the schools started by the government were under the direction of the missionaries. Ultimately, the whole educational administrative system was in the hand of the missionaries in the north and south, from April 1, 1904.[147]

One of the main reasons for handing over of educational responsibility to the missionaries was the result of the missionaries' effort and hard work toward education. The missionaries found school education as an important means for spreading the Gospel.

During the early period of the establishment of schools, there was no proper systematic formal system of education. However, there were some methods and policies of the mission regarding school education. The fundamental point to be remembered is that the schools functioned under the aid of the government and the management of the missionaries.

Girls schools

In the initial stage, the Mizo boys and girls attended school together. In Northern Mizoram, in the year 1899, there were 6 girls out of 36 students, in the year 1900, there were 11 girls out of 66 students, and in 1901, there were 20 girls out of 180, and in 1902, there were 40 girl students. In the first lower primary examination held in the year 1903, out of 19 students, 2 students were girls, namely, Nu-i and Saii who stood at fifth and seventh position, respectively, in this exam. In 1904, two girls passed the lower primary examination, they were Pawngi and Thangi.[148]

Between the years 1902 and 1903, temporary schools were started in three villages for the Mizo girls. It is worthy to note that the teachers were Mizo women who passed the lower primary examination.[149] Then in 1904, in Aizawl, permanent girls' school was started by Mrs. K.E. Jones.[150] In the southern part, girls boarding was properly started as early as 1908.[151] Since then, the girl's schools were developed passing through up and down situations.

The mission school made an effort and played a role in the uplift of the Mizo women. Mizo women were subordinates in traditional society. In Mizo history, mission school education laid the foundation for changing the status of women in Mizo society. This will be dealt with in more detail in the next chapter.

Boarding Schools

The general standard of the Mizo students was very low due to irregular attendance. Some of the factors as mentioned by J.V Hluna are: one of the main factors was their nomadic life. In addition to their migration habit, their occupation was another factor responsible for low standard of Mizo students. Their parents let them work in the fields during harvest time.

Moreover, some chiefs and many parents were not aware of the necessity of educating their children.[152] Therefore, for the improvement of the attendance and the quality of their students, the mission planned to have a boarding school at Serkawn and Aizawl.[153]

The Superintendent Major Cole also had the same desire; he, therefore, discussed it with the leaders of Welsh Calvinistic Methodist in 1905.[154] With a small amount granted by the government, the mission completed the construction of hostels in Aizawl and in Lunglei, where 70 persons each could be accommodated. In the construction work, there was a significant contribution by the natives as manual work was done free of cost. Money was spent only on skilled labor and materials.[155] In 1907, the mission at Lunglei had also started an experimental girls' boarding school with great success.[156]

As expected, the mission boarding school soon became the center of education. A good number of teachers, evangelists, and government employees were produced from boarding schools. One interesting thing was that in the hostel, the students had done all the necessary things like cooking, fetching water, and collecting firewood. The girls took responsibility for doing all the works connected with their establishment, and the boys looked after theirs.[157] There was thus no need to employ sweepers, peons, washmen, or firewood carriers.[158] All the boarders took part in whatever was necessary to be done.

In light of the new education system, one can see the image of the traditional system of education, where boys and girls were trained in *Zawlbuk* and in family, respectively, in the administration of the hostel. As the *Zawlbuk* was the central place of education before the establishment of formal education, the boarding school was an alternative to the *Zawlbuk* education. The content of the Mizos traditional education and the mission school was different in some aspects but moral conduct and physical training still continued to be an important content of the boarding school education.

Establishment of High School

Since 1926, there was a demand from the people to open a high school. The Welsh Mission also made an attempt to open a high school., however, the government did not permit it. The high schools were started only in 1944.[159] Therefore, those who passed the middle standard needed to go to high schools outside Mizoram. Again in 1929, the mission made an effort to open high schools but the superintendent prohibited it.[160]

In spite of the demands for high school, the government was reluctant to establish as it was not interested in promoting the Mizos to hold higher status in government jobs. The late establishment of the high schools in Mizoram reflects the attitude of the government officials over the Mizo people. The Mizos were suppressed from getting high positions for jobs in the government. Here, it is interesting to note that the government policy and the mission policy with regard to education in Mizoram are contrary to each other in some areas particularly in the establishment of high schools. While the missionaries made an effort to establish high school, the government officials did not easily permit them. However, due to a strong demand by the natives, it was finally established in 1944 after the outbreak of the world war.

5. The Content/Curriculum of the Mission School

It is not possible to discuss in detail, the entire curriculum of the mission school education between the year 1904 and 1952 as there was a development as it was reported by Savidges in

1916, "The duties of schoolwork seem to increase in the same proportion as the School boys grow." Every year something fresh has to be added to the curriculum.[161]

The Initial Phase (1894–1903)

The primary aim of the missionaries was to spread the Gospel among the Hill people through their school curriculum. Thus, biblical subject occupied the central part. D.E. Jones reported thus "A prominent place is given to biblical teaching in the schools, but other branches of the elementary education cannot be excluded."[162] In the early part of the establishment of the mission schools, emphasis was given to teach reading and writing. One of the textbooks called *Zirtirh Bu* (A Lushai Primer) published in the year 1895 was the first book, which was written in Mizo language. Unfortunately, the copy is not available at present.[163]

The first textbook was mainly used for learning reading and writing and it comprised mainly the alphabet in capital letter and in small letter. In 1901, *Zirtirh Bu* was again published, which comprised of 27 pages. In this textbook, we find the continuity of teaching the Mizo traditional moral value. The proverbs like "Do not steal," "do not harm others," "respect your mother and father," (trns. by the author), etc. The enclosure of short maxims in the textbook reflected the desire of continuing the Mizo sayings as the means of imparting moral conduct among the Mizo.

Due to the increase in attendance, in 1900, the mission school was divided into two sections elementary and advance. The elementary section was held in the morning and the advance section in the daytime. The advance section was taught courses like *Lushai composition, Geography, Arithmetic, English, Teaching Methods, and Acts of the Apostles.* The Lushai composition consisted of writing the history of their native religion-demons, God, and also Christian subjects.[164] In 1903, the first lower primary examination was held and 13 students of the mission school wrote the exam and all of them passed this exam.

In the initial stage, the content of the mission school mainly focused on how to read and write at the same time, the curriculum comprised of some portions of the Gospel. Therefore, the traditional method of education like oratory was replaced by the written form and the Mizo learned how to read and write by a new alphabet. Although there was a change in the system, we also find the continuity of core content of traditional education, which was *the moral conduct.*

Period of Consolidated (1904–1934)

The period between 1904 and 1926 can be said as the consolidated period for the mission school in terms of the establishment of different classes and curriculum. Upper primary was introduced and the first examination was held in 1904 in north Mizoram and in 1905 in the south. The subjects were Reading, Composition, Grammar, Arithmetic, Account, mental Arith., History, and Euclids (Geometry).[165] The Middle English Schools were started in 1907 at Aizawl and in 1914 at Serkawn. These were the only Middle English Schools in Mizoram till 1944.[166] The content and curriculum of the mission school during this consolidating period can be described as follows.

School: Center of Religious Teaching

After careful observation, Rochunga Pudaite gives a summary of the aim of education thus:

> Education was aimed strictly at religious instruction. The people were taught the three R's[167] in preparation for Bible reading and understanding of writing and simple arithmetic for religious exercises... with their conversion to Christianity, primary emphasis was placed upon their ability to read the Bible.[168]

In the primary school syllabus, many Bible passages, Christian songs, and choruses were included as part of the regular course of study. From the 1916 report, one can learn that in the lower primary course, the scripture, the Gospel of St. Mark carried 75 marks and Christian hymns carried 15 marks out of a total of 370. In the upper primary examination, the scripture carried 75 marks out of 495.[169] The daily classes began with devotions and ended with Christian songs of prayers.[170] During the 1910s, special attention was paid to reading and writing, reading aloud was practiced by the students so that the students could read the Bible to their people in the church and in the villages.[171] Teaching doctrines and some portion of the Bible were compulsory in the mission schools too.

In the Mizo traditional education, the core content of its education was moral values, which concerned more with the welfare of society. However, the mission school can be claimed as the center for Christian value teaching. It also can be said as it was a center of religious teaching, the moral conduct of the Mizo was replaced by the teaching of Christian values. However, though there was a transition from cultural value to Christian values, it was complementary to each other. The Mizo *Tlawmngaihna* or Mizo moral conduct was not opposite to the Christian moral values.

Continuation of the Mizo Traditional Values

The western missionaries also believed that school education should not be isolated from the basic cultural heritage of the Mizos, and that education would be of real value only out of their native cultural inheritance. In 1904, two conferences, with a concern for the improvement of the curriculum, were held at Aizawl. The Baptist and the Welsh Presbyterian missionaries unanimously decided that "Old Lushai Custom should be preserved".[172] Therefore, there was an effort to preserve and keep the old Mizo custom through school curriculum. The following aspects are pointed out to find out whether there was continuity in teaching the Mizo traditional values.

(a) Mizo Legends and Short Stories

As a result of the 1904 conferences, Mizo legends and short stories were included in the curriculum. In the Middle English School, the syllabus included "The Legend of Old *Lushais*" a collection of Mizo legends, like—two *Chhurbura thawnthu* (the story of a man called Chhurbura), the story of *Tlumtea*, the story of *Vaichaka*, and the stories of *Tualvungi* were translated into English.[173] In primary school, it was also included the Mizo history and relationships with their neighbors.[174]

(b) Mizo Sayings or Proverbs

The Lushai Primer (the textbook used for students studying in lower primary) that was prepared by Edwin Rowlands in 1926 also included 12 Mizo sayings or proverbs for instance "*A tha lam kawng a chho a, a chhe lam kawng a phei,*" *The road of the good is narrow and difficult but leads to life, while the road of the bad is broad and easy but leads to destruction.*

"*Mahni infak leh Sakhi ngalah engmah a bet lo,*" meaning, just as there is no flesh on the leg of a deer, there is no worth in self-praise.

"*Lungpui pawh lungtein a kamki loh chuan a awm thei lo,*" literally means "A huge stone could not stand without leaning against a small stone." It means that everyone is equally important in one's respective place regardless of one's personal disposition and abilities.

"*Vawina tih tur naktuka tihah khek suh*," which means "do not leave anything unfinished what you ought to complete today." The 12 points of "Good Conduct" were included like "Well begin must be learned in every way," "Do everything at a right time and keep everything in the right place," "older people must be honored and respected," etc. Besides these, in "The Lushai Primer" the name of the birds and the names of the wild animals which existed in the Mizo villages were included. It also described the method of the Mizo jhum cultivation. It further included the names of trees, and one song that described the "love of mother."

The moral values that were taught in the traditional Mizo society also occupied an important place in formal education. We can see thus the continuity of the teaching of moral conduct in the mission school.

(c) Practical Works

In 1910, the government introduced "Gardening" into the curriculum of the primary schools of Assam. Some teachers tried the same in Mizoram but it caused a decrease in attendance in Aizawl.[175] It is difficult to know the reason for this. However, in Serkawn, Gardening was successfully done as reported by F.W Savidge.[176] Basket-weaving by using Cane and Bamboo was introduced as early as 1916 for the students' practical work.[177] In 1925, cane and bamboo work was added in the syllabus.[178]

This practical work seems to be not a new item for the Mizo children as they were familiar with crop cultivation. However, flower gardening was not commonly practiced among the Mizo, particularly by the boys.

Western Values

The missionaries made a decision "to preserve the Old Lushai custom" but it can be said that this was not their main aim in education. Their main aim of mission school education was for evangelization. However, English short stories were also included. In the textbook "Lushai Middle Reader: In Printing Part I," we find the story of Edward VII & Queen Alexandra, Mary Moffat, etc.[179] In some of the textbooks, the colonial ideas of imperialism were also imparted. Some important examples can be pointed out as follows:

First, the 26th edition of the *Zirtirh Bu Thar* (New Lushai Primer) found the counteract of the cultural aspect of the Mizos. In English version, it goes like this "In the early period of the Mizos, there was no particular tribes of Chiefs, every Mizo tribe had their own Chief."[180] There was a strong reaction from the Sailo Chiefs against this statement. In 1941, there was a meeting of the Sailo Chiefs at Aizawl. They discussed this matter and took measures to have it excluded from the textbook. The common understanding of the Mizos is that there were many Chiefs in the Lushai hills. The Chieftainship was inherited and the Sailo tribe was one of the popular tribes among the Mizo chiefs.[181]

However, the statement in the textbook of the mission school changed the contemporary Mizos' perception with regard to this aspect. The Mizo historian B. Lalthangliana also finds it difficult to ascertain which of the beliefs is more reliable.[182]

Second, in the textbook of 1901 prepared by Edwin Rowlands, it was written that there were five major races in the world, black, brown, yellow, red, and white but we all are of the same.[183] In 1916 in the same textbook revised by D.E Jones, there was an additional sentence, in English translation it goes like this: "… there are five major races… black, brown, yellow, red and white but we all are same. The yellow race is the most populated, the whites are the wisest and the powerful."[184]

Here there is an important issue; does this imply that D.E Jones wanted to impart this to make the Mizos accept the value or the superiority of the white people over all races? Was it one of the reasons that increased the Mizos' admiration of the white people? B. Lalthangliana also observed that some of the phrases which were included in the text book could be one of the deeply rooted influencing factors of the profound admiration of the white people by the Mizos; who till today look up to the western way of living and imitate their lifestyle.[185] After Indian independence, the phrase was struck off from the textbook in 1959.[186]

It is also necessary to note that in the earlier textbook, which was prepared by Edwin Roland, there was not such a phrase. Therefore, it can be assumed that among the missionaries, there were different attitudes toward the native people in imparting value system.

In the textbook published in 1926 that was prepared by D.E. Jones, we also find the names of the months (January–December) written in English.[187] However, it seems that the name of the months in Mizo language was also added in the later period.[188] While the Mizo had their own way of naming the months in a year,[189] the English name of the months was taught in the school textbook in the early period. This would be the reason that, presently, most Mizos are not able to recite the name of the months in a year in Mizo. In general, using the name of the month in Mizo language is replaced by the English name of the months in a year.

Third, one of the textbooks *Thu-Ro-Bu* (The treasury, an advanced reader for Lushai schools) prepared by D.E. Jones and

Edwin Rowland comprises of different topics. It contained 164 pages. Half of the lesson was concerned about the Christian teaching. Besides Christian teaching, it also included the story of Queen Victoria, John Franklin, and Newton, etc. One topic written by Edwin Rowland was "The Government,"[190] which mainly focuses on the privilege of loyalty to the government.

During this period, the Mizo perception of the administration of the government was that the "government was a burden for Mizos" because the government collected revenue, it also collected their guns, it introduced forced labor and there were many manual labor work.[191]

Therefore, it seems that through this writing, the missionaries tried to influence the Mizos by teaching that if they paid the tax in reverse, there would be development in dispensary and schools. It is also interesting to underline such statements in this topic: "raided in the Lushai hills were ceased and there was peaceful condition because of the present of government military..."[192] It can be seen that the idea of imperialism was imparted through the textbook. In this way, one can witness the sense of superiority the missionaries felt with the Mizos.

Fourth, music, no other than western-type music was also introduced by the missionaries. Singing played an important part in academic life. Group singing was popular and school student formed choir and always sang in church conference.[193] J.V Hluna also said that students of Serkawn and Aizawl Mission Schools were well versed in tonic-solfa.[194] Therefore, the western way of singing and participation of the groups in worship service were the prototypes of the western music.

Thus, a foreign language and foreign music were simultaneously introduced in the mission school. The traditional music tunes were replaced by the western style of music and the tune of the songs. In fact, this could be one of the reasons that after a later period, there was a big issue within the Church in accepting the Mizo traditional tune. In the 1990s when Christian song composers composed Christian songs with the Mizo traditional tune even if they were Gospel-centered lyrics, many elders could not accept such songs to be sung in the Church worship service.[195]

Finally, during this period, Middle English School was started in 1907 in Aizawl and in 1914 at Serkawn. The English language forms an important part of the course, and in the highest classes, it was used as a medium of instruction.[196] Thus, English became a more and more the important means of instruction in the school. Therefore, the importance of the English language was also imposed as early as the 1910s among the Mizo.

One of the probable reasons for imposing English as the medium of education from the middle school stage in India and also in Mizoram reflected the political interest in unifying the emotions and ambitions of the colonized people. English education was introduced as one of the means of colonization of the sociocultural aspects of the native people. In his famous thesis, Thomas Macaulay opined that the English education would play a significant role in cultural influence and this will further transform the Indians loyal to the British.[197] He further wrote, "once the cultural changed was achieved, the Indian people will stop to fight for independence. The native shall not rise against us and thus the energy will be fully and harmlessly employed in acquiring and resolving European knowledge and in adapting European institutions."[198] The majorities of educational missionaries were influenced or went in line with Macaulay's idea. Thus, for the missionaries, the teaching of the Bible and English language was inseparable.

However, as Aloysius Pieres rightly said about the significance of language, "language is not just a medium of communication or a symbol of civility but an experience of reality. The language they speak puts them in touch with the basic truths that every religion grapple with."[199] Lawmsanga also states,

> The language also determines the explanation or understanding of the truth and thus directs the social praxis to realize the perceived truth explanations. Furthermore, language is a medium of one's own social reality, the reality of life. Therefore, alienation from the social self was the immediate outcome of imposing an alien language English in missionary education. Moreover, depriving people of their mother tongue resulted in their alienation from the truth of life, creating a structural inability in them to search for the fundamentals of their own reality.[200]

While the curriculum of mission school education in Mizoram was Christian oriented, simultaneously, the western values appeared in the curriculum of the mission school education. However, it is unresolved whether the missionaries, intensionally or unintentionally included such imperialistic ideas in the school text book. Students were taught and instructed in such ways to become faithful Christians as well as future leaders of the church. The students were mainly oriented to spread the Gospel through the teaching of how to read and write. They were also taught to be loyal to the government and to be faithful citizens under the British Government.

Reforming the System of Education (1935–1952)

The Superintendent and the missionaries felt the need to follow the same curriculum in the whole of Mizoram. For this concern, a conference was held at Aizawl in 1935. In this meeting, W.H. Carter, the Honorary Inspector of Schools for the south and Rev. D. Edwards, the Honorary Inspector of Schools for the north were also present under the leadership of Major MacCall,

Superintendent of the Lushai hills.[201] The conference launched a comprehensive scheme for the improvement of education. The reason for reorganization of the system and curriculum can be understood by the report given by H.W. Carter:

> For a number of years, it has been obvious that in boys' post-primary education in Lushai emphasis has been on wrong subjects. The middle English course has been chiefly a stepping stone to the high school, [the Mizo usually join high school in Shillong], whence boys have returned eminently fitted for salaried posts, but totally unsuited for a return to village life if salaried post were not forthcoming. How few such posts are in the hill districts of Assam I myself did not realize until I heard at Shillong the Deputy Commissioner of the Garo Hills say that the government offices in his district could absorb only matriculate in five years! Openings for boys with high school training are probably no more plentiful in Lushais yet at this moment more than Lushais are studying high schools. The danger we in Lushai have so far avoided, of having a disgruntled, unemployed matriculate class, is now at our door. The remedy is to remove the emphasis from Middle English Course to Middle Vernacular course, which will aim at the teaching only those subjects which will help Lushai boys to live a normal yet enlightened village life. The "Eight year plan" therefore provides for the setting up of four Middle Vernacular, in addition to new, primary schools to bring the total to 50.[202]

As the outcome of the conference, the authorities of both south and north Mizoram decided to maintain uniformity in all possible scopes of education. Therefore, from 1936, a common curriculum was established in the north and south, and the first common examination was held in 1936.[203] In fact, not only in its uniformity in the curriculum but also in the mission school entered a new phase in administrative function.

As a result of the conference, both the mission in the north and south, Presbyterian Church and Baptist Church, respectively, formed the Education Management Committee in 1936. It was in order to create a better relationship between the mission education work and the Mizo churches.[204] Before the formation of the Education Management Committee, all the authorities of the school were vested with the missionaries. The church did not involve in the management of school education.[205] However, since 1936, the churches in the north and the south took deeper responsibility along with the missionaries.

It can also be said that though the Mizo teachers made a great contribution to the development of the mission school before 1936, they were not involved in the management committee. The missionaries alone took up all the authority for a long period of time.

During this phase, the Mizoram education system was focusing on vernacular education. On the recommendation of the Joint Educational Conference, 9 middle vernaculars were opened in the subsequent year of 1936. 2 Middle English Schools were increased to 5 M.E. School[206] and 9 Middle Vernacular schools increased to 10 Middle Vernacular till India became independent.[207]

In 1942, as a result of the submission of a proposal by the Superintendent of the Lushai Hills to the Governor of Assam on approval of the Government, "The Lushai Hills District Education Board" was formed, which was composed of missionaries from the north and south. High school was established in 1944. On January 4, 1952, Mizoram got an autonomous District Council. In the same year, school education responsibility was handed over to the government.[208]

Concerning the curriculum, games, nature study, Scripture, storytelling, clay modeling, and health teaching were also included in the kindergarten.[209] The primary curriculum included Vernacular, English, Arithmetic, Geography of the Lushai Hills and Assam, Scripture, Hygiene, Nature study,

Music, Drawing, physical training, and handwork.[210] The Middle English Curriculum included Vernacular, English, Arithmetic, Geography, History of India, Scripture, Hygiene, Drawing, Painting, and Handwork.[211] From the curriculum, it can be learned that practical aspects were more focused than in the previous phases. One of the important elements of the girls' school was the introduction of weaving of rugs out of Lushai cotton. The report given by Miss Katie Hughes in 1939 is as follows:

> In the Girls' School this year we were asked to weave rugs out of Lushai cotton, so we decided to have a cotton project… We found out how much we should need to weave twelve rugs calculating the measurements and cost. Nearly all their Arithmetic syllabus for the year was covered in this way…Before reaching the rug stage the cotton had to be put through several different processes by the children starting from class one up. The actual weaving of the rug was done by class six, and they were all accepted as first grade rugs. As there is no prospect of work for girls that leave school the girls can now weave rug at home with their own cotton, sell them, and in this way help their family. This was our first project and the teacher and girls entered into venture with great enthusiasm.[212]

We see the continuity of the practical aspect of the mission school education. However, the changes during this period confronted many issues. One of the important issues was that of the focus on the middle vernacular. As mentioned earlier, the government did not pay much attention to develop higher education.

Although the missionaries requested permission for opening high school, the establishment of high school was also not permitted for a long period of time. However, students who passed Middle English joined high school in other places. One of the serious questions was why did the government suddenly change the system of education? Was the government not interested in giving the Mizo higher education? It seemed so. Saprawnga[213] strongly argued that the government was not interested in higher education. Saprawnga expressed his opinion saying,

> Concerning education in Mizoram the British official were in dilemma, they feel the need of educating the Mizo but they were afraid that Mizo will pursue higher standard. Therefore, they cleverly made an obstacle for pursuing higher education by limiting the standard up to Middle English for a long period of time... moreover during 1930s they even replaced the Middle English school by Middle Vernacular. They cleverly planed that the course of Middle Vernacular not to be fit for joining High school. The Mizo protested against this system and many people were reluctant to join Middle Vernacular.[214]

With careful observation, it can be understood that the government was not interested in higher education. It is evidenced from the very little expenditure of the government allocated to fund education in Mizoram as Mac Call says: "The cost incurred by the government on education of Lushai has never exceeded three halfpence per head of population per year with the first 40 years of British administration."[215] Moreover, the rapid growth of literacy in Mizoram was found after 1941. The percentage of the literacy growth in 1941 was 19.50%, after independence in 1951, it was 31.13%, and in 1961, it was 44.00% and even in 1971, it rose to 53.79% of the total population.[216] This shows that the Mizos were suppressed for their intellectual development during the colonial rule.

6. The Inconsistency between Mission Education and Mizo Culture

When the traditional Mizo society interacted with the system of mission school education, there were many rough spots in the process of the establishment of education in Mizoram.

Female Education

At first, many menfolk opposed education for girls, whom they considered inferior. According to H.S. Sawiluaia, one of the main reasons for opposing girls' education by the parents was that girls were too useful at home. Another reason was that parents were anxious that girls would make use of their literacy for sending love letters to boys.[217] J.H. Lorrain writes in his report in 1913:

> Female education in South Lushai is a problem which has yet to be solved. Lushai girls from the time she is about 4 years of age begins to help her mother. This she does first by minding the baby, and later on by also carrying small loads of firewood from the forest, or bamboo tubes of water from the spring. While her brothers of twice and thrice her age are spending their days playing in the village streets or snaring birds in the jungle, she is constantly busy and is so useful to her poor hard-worked mother that she cannot possibly be spared to come to school. This is the chief reason why we have been able to get so few girls boarders. We have a girls hostel capable of accommodating a matron and some 12 to 15 pupils; but up to the present that good woman has only 3 girls under her care. We hope for better success that this in the near future.[218]

The missionaries asked permission from the government to exempt "forced labor" by the parents from those who sent their children to attend school. There was much correspondence in this regard. Lorrain's application shows an attempt to increase daily attendance with the exemption from forced labor:[219] From the letter, it can also be noticed that in the past, the government had executed "exemption of 'forced labor' upon the parents of the boys at boarding school."[220]

From the correspondences between the missionaries and the government officials, it is interesting to note that in the past, the government had granted a special privilege to the parents of boys who pass the upper primary examination. Therefore, to increase the number of girls in the schools, Lorrain requested the government officials to grant "*Kuli awl*" (exemption of forced labor) for the parents who send their girl children to their school. It is also interesting to note that Lorrain's application was not granted.[221]

From the missionaries side, they tried to uplift women's status by giving regular education. They may justify themselves by saying that they made a big effort in favor of the Mizo girls. however, the attitude of the missionaries and system of the mission schools in relation to the Mizo women should be critically evaluated. In the report, J.H. Lorrain says:

> Several women and girls living on or near the Mission Station have been coming to Mrs. Savidge (and more lately to Mrs. Lorrain) for lessons in reading and s sewing. Although they have not always been able to attend regularly, on account of their domestic duties and arduous field work, they have made a good progress. Some of them have succeeded in mastering the art of reading and have been rewarded by the gift of a bound volume of scripture portions.[222]

It is evidenced that women were extremely worked hard in traditional Mizo society and they were very useful at home. It is seen that without regular attendance and with their domestic and fieldwork, they could catch up with what were taught. The missionaries, however, tried to implement the western system of education with a proper function in discipline and administration with regular attendance. However, the economic condition and the living standard of the western people and the traditional Mizos society were incomparable.

Therefore, from the Mizo situational point of view, there was a lack of contextualization of the system and methods of education to meet the need of women education. It does not mean that all the education systems should be completely adjusted in line with the culture of a people; the intention here is that in the situation of the girls in Mizo society, the expectation of the missionaries was far above the ground reality.

Obstacles from the Chief and the Elders

In the initial period of the introduction of schools in Mizoram, some Mizo chiefs objected as they saw it as a threat to their traditional authority. It can be seen in the *Mizo leh Vai Chanchinbu* (monthly journal) in 1904 written by Chhunthangvunga saying, In the previous year, we tried to influence two of the villages' chiefs named Dokhama and Lianhnawla to establish school in their villages. But the elders and the chiefs of the two villages did not permit to construct the school building saying that the "teachers will replace the authority of the Chief."

However, after they were enlightened that it was for the benefit of the society they allowed the establishment of the school in their village (translated from Mizo version).[223] There was suspicion by some chiefs and some elders that the authority of the chief would be replaced by the teachers in village administration, therefore there were some of chiefs who did not welcome education in their village. C. Nunthara also says:

> In the initial period, Christianity made little headway among the chiefs, and the elders and their followers, and these people remained adamant, for a long period of time, to send their children to mission schools because they believed that Christianity and the new education would do away with their traditional power and authority.[224]

Therefore, mission school education indirectly, on the one hand, played an important role in decreasing or devaluing the authority of the Chief in different villages. No one seemed to care how hard it must have been for the Mizo Chiefs, the disgrace they must have felt when their power was stripped from them during the transitional period. Instead, they blamed the chiefs for not willing to let the school be established in their village. However, as people of different villages were influenced to enroll their children, the chiefs and the elders had no power to resist

Christianity and education in Mizoram rather in the later period seeing the advantages of education in terms of government jobs and intellectual development, the chiefs were no longer opposed to school education as the influence of education in Mizo society was inexorable.

Inconsistency with Occupation

The main occupation of the Mizos was shifting cultivation. Due to their method of cultivation, the Mizo frequently migrated from one place to another looking for more productive land for their cultivation. This happened to be one of the obstacles to the development of the mission schools in Mizoram. Mr. Savides writes:

> Although some of the village schools have had to be changed on account of the villagers migrating to new sites, the work has been encouraging. It is difficult to establish schools in villages, for as soon as teaching has just begun to pass the elementary stages, the people move to a new spot more profitable for their cultivation. There is a strong desire among the lads to learn, but the parents often oppose that desire because they lost their children's help at weeding and sowing. They understand the advantage of education, but they are not yet prepared to make any sacrifice for the sake of their offspring.[225]

J.M. Lloyd also made a comment saying—"All sorts of explanatory circumstances were occasions for absence of students which had not many parallels in other parts of India."[226] Because of the nature of occupation, school attendance usually got low during harvest season. Besides the harvest work, Mizo children were deeply engaged with the family household work like looking for missing domestic animals, repairing the fencing of the vegetable garden.[227] The basic factor responsible for irregularity of the attendance in the school was that the value of education was not yet deeply rooted among the Mizos in the initial period.

Therefore, in order to encourage regularity in school attendance, the missionaries introduced prizes of soap and combs at the end of the year to those who had the best record of attendance.[228] However, lack of knowledge of the social life and customs of the Mizos on part of the missionaries also caused some problems.

One of the examples may be cited here—a student in Aizawl once asked the headmaster Rev. E.L. Mendus for special leave to go home to his village for some days. When the student was asked for the reason, the student told the headmaster that his father was going to make a feast by killing a pig. The headmaster discovered that it was not the students' real father who intended to organize the feast but his uncle. Therefore, he considered it as unreasonable and was not inclined to grant the leave. However, after further inquiry, he realized that the occasion that was to be celebrated was an extremely important event in the family, and also came to know how close-knitted sisters and brothers were in a Mizo family. The fathers' brother was often called a "father" among the Mizos and that the uncle sometimes occupied a position of equal importance to that of the father. Thus, the headmaster had to grant permission for leave to the student.[229]

Irregular attendance of the Mizo in the school was not because of an unreasonable excuse but it was a reasonable problem. J.V. Hluna has also said that there was no such problem in discipline of the student as the spirit of *Tlawmngaihna*, which always demanded a highly desirable conduct, was deeply rooted in the mind of the Mizos. The problems of discipline in the school did not pose any great difficulties.[230] Mendus also said that the problem of discipline does not appear to present as much difficulties as one might anticipate.[231] Therefore, lack of situational understanding by the missionaries also created problems in the administration of education.

Conclusion

With the advent of the missionaries, traditional form of education was replaced by formal education. In the process of transition of the traditional education to formal education, one remarkable aspect was the formulation of the Mizo alphabet, which was prepared by the two pioneer missionaries with the help of Suaka and Thangphunga. It is also worthy to note the formulation of the Mizo's alphabet, and the use of native language as a medium of instruction was initiated by the two missionaries.

The government administration to some extent supported the missionaries and made a significant contribution to the native people in the field of education. However, as the government was reluctant to provide higher level of standard education, there is a question of why the government was not interested in providing higher education in schools for the Mizos. It can be said that the British Government did not give priority to the development of the Mizo community. However, education was also used as a means for developing and sustaining proper administration and governance for the advantage of the British Government among the hill tribes.

There was also development in curriculum and content of the mission school education since 1894. Since the initial stage, the principle or the core content of the mission school was imparting Christian values. There was common ground between the core and principle of traditional education and formal education because the moral conduct of the traditional Mizo society and Christian values complimented each other. It is also evidenced from the analysis of the textbooks and curriculum that there was also continuity in teaching traditional values. Efforts were also made to preserve old Lushai customs. However, the study reveals that western values were also imparted through textbooks and curriculum. Practical aspects like cane and bamboo work, weaving, and gardening were added in the curriculum. One of the peculiarities of the mission school to the Mizos was women's education, which became a means of transformation in the status of women in Mizoram. However, in the transitional period of traditional education to formal education, there were many obstacles to the process development of formal education.

Since the beginning of the establishment of the mission school, the Mizo society was making a new chapter in its history. The mission school played a significant role in various aspects of the Mizo society. The role and impact of the mission school will be dealt with in the next chapter to understand the changes led by the school education in Mizo society.

Chapter 3

The Role and Impact of Mission Schools in the Transformation of Traditional Mizo Society

In the previous chapter, the origin and the development of mission school education in Mizoram have been analyzed. In this chapter, the focus will be on the role and impact of the mission school on Mizo society. Mission school had a significant impact on the sociocultural and religious life of the Mizos. The leading questions in this chapter will be: What is the role of the mission school? What are the impacts of the mission school in Mizoram?

1. Social Transformation

The mission school played a significant role in the transformation of the traditional Mizo society. The following historically important points are taken up for detailed analysis.

Paradigm Shift in the Key Figure in the Village

The development of the alphabet and the reduction of language into written form have played a vital role in this process of transformation of communication and consequently, in the very culture of people itself. The rapid increase in the literacy rate since the beginning of the establishment of school education is the witness of new values aspect, which was that the literate person was developed among the Mizos.

The following data[232] show the rapid increase in literacy rate in Mizoram.

Table 2 Population of Mizoram showing Christian population and literacy rate 1901–1991

Year	Population in Mizoram	Christian population	Literacy rate	Growth of literacy rate in percentage
1901	82,434	45 (0.05%)	771 (.93%)	
1911	91,204	2,461 (2.77 %)	3,635 (4.41%)	377.16
1921	98,406	27,720 (28.17 %)	6,183 (6.28%)	70.10
1931	124,404	59,123 (47.52 %)	13,320 (10.54%)	147.10
1941	152,786	98,108 (64.21 %)	29,765 (19.50%)	124.46
1951	196,202	157,575 (80.31 %)	61,039 (31.13%)	105.25
1961	266,063	230,509 (86.64%)	117,094 (44.00%)	91.66
1971	332,390	286,141 (86.09%)	178,793 (53.79%)	52.69
1981	493,757	413,840 (84.00%)	295,685 (59.88%)	65.37
1991	689, 756	591,342 (85.73%)	461,930 (82.27%)	82.27

From the above data, it is clear that the growth of literacy rate in Mizoram was very fast. The highest growth of literacy rate in percentage falls under the year between 1901 and 1911. One of the important factors of the rapid growth of literacy rate in Mizoram is that the valuable contribution made by the Mizos themselves. According to Lloyd, "As soon as a few of them had attained literacy the Mizo began to help others to read and write so that in a very short time there were at least one or two in every village who had the skill to read."[233] As one of the main aims of the missionaries was to lead the Mizo to read the Bible, people responded to it enthusiastically and in an unprecedented way.

As we have already seen, missionaries and Christianity played a dominant role in it. However, the most historically significant part, which has been sidelined in many researches and writings, is the role of the local people. Therefore, all the credits cannot be given only to the missionaries. Both the natives and the missionaries played a significant role. The natives who taught their fellow friends not only in the school education but also outside the school especially in the early period of the establishment of school education were, in fact, the core factor in the rapid growth of literacy rate in Mizoram. As shown in the table, the growth of literacy of the Mizo and the rate of literacy in Mizoram increased from 2.95% in 1901 to 51.24% in 1961.

There were many developments due to intellectual transformation in Mizo society. Women were uplifted through education. It has its advantages in spreading the Gospel through Bible reading communication, information could be done by writing. However, during the transition period of preliterate to literate period, it can be rightly assumed that there was a division among the Mizos into two broad groups, namely, the literate and illiterate groups. Moreover, the traditional value system of the village changed because of education. After the establishment of formal schools in Mizoram, the literates were more respected in the villages while in the traditional Mizo society, elders or *Val Upa* were more respectable persons. It can be rightly imagined how fast the younger would easily catch up how to read and write easily, while for the older in age, it was difficult. Therefore, education became one of the means of transformation and, moreover, the role played by *Valupa* was extended beyond the role of the teacher. However, the beautiful manner of giving respect to elders in the Mizo society also declined in the contemporary Mizo society.[234] Education deeply played an important impact in this regard. For instance, highly educated persons were valued in the Mizo society.

This reality further reflected back on the value system of the Mizo. The decisive factors surrounding outstanding persons were also changing in Mizo society. In traditional society whoever performed *thangchhuah* and heroic acts were highly valued. However, they were no longer valued in contemporary Mizo society.

In the book entitled *Tun Kum za chhunga Mizo Hnam puipate 1894-1994* (*The Outstanding Leaders During This Century, 1894-1994*) written by C. Vanlawma, the writer selected 100 people as the outstanding leaders or people among the Mizos and also he included 10 English men and he wrote their short biographies. When critically examined how he wrote their short biography, it can be learned that their skill in education is one of the credits given by C. Vanlawma and almost all of them were educated persons.[235] Rev. Lalnghinglova also narrated the importance of the mission school teachers saying that whenever the letter was sent by the teacher, they wrote their title "*Ztu*" (short forms of Teacher in Mizo language) in the beginning of their name to indicate that they are not ordinary persons. They were honored and admired persons in the village. He further said during their time, the teachers were given higher privilege than the present days of graduates (BA). "Thus said the teacher" was more effective than today's "thus said the Deputy Commissioners."[236]

In fact, it is evidenced from the discussion that teachers held a high status in Mizo society during the transition period from preliterate society to literate society. One of the core factors for this was the traditional practices that were transformed. The teachers were no more recognized and praised by their *Tlawmngaihna* rather they were recognized by their educational qualification. The observation of missionaries also can be seen as early as 1936:

> …Education has become one of the accepted "values" of Lushai life. In the old days, "value" was summed up in the sense of achievement brought by performing certain sacrifices, and to the processor of gun. But one of the great desires nowadays is to be educated.[237]

The value system that was highly regarded in traditional Mizo society was gradually changed by the value of western system of education in Mizoram.

The Role of Native Teachers

The missionaries were convinced from the beginning that they needed to open schools to train a few of the ablest students to be "teachers." This fact was supported by the words of the missionaries; "school was opened by us with a view to train a few of the most forward scholars to be teachers."[238] In southern Mizoram, therefore, Savidge's educational method was to train those who had learned to read and write from the government schools and were preparing to become teachers. Those were given the responsibility of teaching those who were still new to the mission school.[239] Thus, Savidge organized the students around a monitorial system that proved to be a very successful approach. Therefore, there were two categories of teachers.

(a) Volunteer Teachers

There were teachers without salary. They taught the village people voluntarily without pay. The missionaries sent them to other villages to teach the people to read and write. Among them, they were people who were not yet Christians. Those volunteer teachers covered more than five villages, namely, Tanhril, Lungleng, Khawrihnim, Phulpui, and Biate and others in teaching the people to read and write.[240] Rev. D.E. Jones reported:

> ...As there are so many of the children moving to other village after a short stay, I hope that it will not only be a means of spreading knowledge, but preparing the way to establish now schools in several villages. This year for the first time Lushai teachers were sent to conduct schools in other parts of the country for a short period. Thanga, Chonga and Toka were the first teachers to start elementary schools in the villages. There were five others supported by us personally, so that they went without salaries, on trial. They are out in the villages they get their food by public subscription of so many tinfuls of rice, and other food items. Schools had been built at those villages by the villagers some months before.[241]

This reflects the nature of the Mizo culture of *Tlawmngaihna*, which we have discussed in the previous chapter. Without any salary, they taught the people of different villages. Therefore, credit must also be given to the Mizo teachers as there was a significant contribution from the indigenous people in educating their people.

(b) Mission Employee Teachers

There were mission employee teachers. They were paid by the mission. It is necessary to understand that the government grant was taken up by the mission in educational field. They made a great contribution in assisting the pastors in different villages. During this period, the pastors cover vast areas of pastorate as they were less in number. Therefore, the school teachers were backbones of the church in the early period of history of Christianity in Mizoram.[242] Rev. J.M. Lloyd righty expressed that the early Mizo teachers were the foundation of Mizoram.[243] Rowlands expresses how their Mizo students especially those in the higher classes have proved very useful, both in preaching and teaching saying, "The school could not be carried on without paid teachers were it not for their aid—they make excellent teachers."[244]

The second group of teachers—those employed by the mission and appointed to certain villages in 1903, were Dorikhuma, Chhunruma, and Hrangsaipuia. After them, Viakhawla, Lianhnuna, Chalkunga, Tumbila, and Dohnuna were appointed. The first generation of mission teachers was one of the most important foundations of the Church in Mizoram as well as the society. Their work, apart from teaching, consisted of preaching the Gospel, planting churches as well as looking after these churches.[245] Frequently they were traveling for preaching the Gospel in far-off places.

By 1927, mission teachers received training at the Mission station in Aizawl.[246] The training was a 1-year course. The first Mizo teacher in the mission's teachers training center was Pasena.[247] Williams gives us a clear picture on how the mission teachers were trained in his report, which reads:

> Besides studying the Theory and Method of teaching they had an opportunity of doing practical teaching in a vacant school near here which can be visited day by day…. They received some theological training in the Theological School here, so that they might be able to lead with the Sunday Schools and other meetings.[248]

Pasena,[249] the first Mizo teacher in the teacher training center made a great contribution to the field of education in Mizoram. He was the son of Dotinchawna, one of the elders and a close friend of chief Lungleng village. He was born in 1893 just before the arrival of the missionaries. His mother died when he was only 5 years. He was looked after by the missionaries and grew up in their home. He passed class 7 from Silchar with financial support from the mission. He worked as the inspector of the school for

3 years (1914–1916). He used to travel to different places to inspect the mission schools. During the First World War in 1917–1818, he went to France and worked as the Head Interpreter. When he came back, Superintendent Major Playfair offered a government job with a higher salary, but Pasena declined it as he preferred working under the mission with lower salary to the government job. He had a privilege to go to London for doing bachelor of teaching. However, he was not qualified for it and he came back with "diploma in education." When he came back, he worked in the teachers' training center. He prepared a number of Mizo school textbooks[250]: C. Vanlawma said Pasena deserves to be called "Father of Mizo Education,"[251] therefore, in the life of Pasena and other Mizo teachers, it can be learned that a significant role is played by Mizo teachers in educating their own people.

The volunteer teachers like Thanga, Chonga, and Toka who initialed elementary schools in the villages without any salary were worthy to be called the foundation of village school in Mizoram. The female voluntary teachers Saii, Pawngi, Nuii are worthy to be honored as they were the forerunners of women education.

Reshaping of the Village Leaders

The school teachers were considered as leaders of the villages and the community.[252] They emerged as the key figures in village life. Their schools were established with the consent of the village chiefs and the villagers. They were recognized by the Government and were supported by the missionaries. Thus, they enjoyed a prominent status in the Mizo society.[253]

According to Lalchhinga as told to him by his father who was one of the advisers to a Chief, the Chief would often seek the advice of the teachers in the administration of his village.[254]

The Chiefs would even want to have school teachers as their elders to help rule the villages. Some of the mission teachers accepted this position while most of them declined the favor. The Chiefs often invited them to attend the village meetings in which they were treated almost like the Chief's Prime Minister if they attend the meeting.[255] Lalnghinglova has given us a description of one such meeting in which the village elders of five villages such as Phulpui, Sateek, Sumsuih, Hmuifang, and Tachhip under one chief called Kamliana met together. A mission teacher Dorikhuma led the meeting. The issues he raised were:

No one should drink liquor, including the chief and his elders, in such meetings.

◊　The meeting should begin with a Bible reading.

◊　The Chief's power should be like that of the British Queen in a meeting.

◊　The Chief should favor his elders.

◊　The Chief should have a good relationship with the Church leaders.[256]

It is evidenced that teachers had great influence on village life. Lloyd rightly comments that they "usually raised the moral tone of a village, guided people away from superstition and provided for many access to the wider world."[257] With regard to point number 2 saying "The Chief should be liked the British Queen," it is difficult to understand what exactly they mean for no document could be found for this clarification. However, it shows that the British Queen or administration system was given a high credit among the Mizo. The above evidence and observations demonstrate wide-ranging impact of education on the value system including ethical, political, and social.

The teachers were expected to do what no one else could do. They represented the development and changes that were taking place in Mizoram. The sacred and secular activities were inextricably linked to them. They were the leaders in both the religious and the social spheres of the villages involving them in all religious and social activities.[258] The teacher also had to be a model in moral aspect as Lloyd rightly says, "Teacher usually raised the moral tone of a village, guided people away from superstition and provide for many an access to the wider world."[259] Jones has given us insights into the teachers' activities from the diary of one village-teacher named Kunga. This is how Kunga describes his own work day by day as cited by D.E. Jones:

> A teacher has to do a lot of unpaid work…. Some of the odd jobs he has to do are to dig a grave…. Make a hoe… help the chief to make a chest… and stay with the mourners. At one time those who stayed to comfort the mourners spent their time telling funny stories, but now the teacher talks about
>
> salvation through Christ…. The teacher may suggest a way of improving the village and may point out some of the bad habits in the village (bad for either health or morals).[260]

The school teachers emerged as a key figure in the village. Therefore, the status and the role of the teachers were a remarkably significant one in the early period of the 20th century in Mizo society. They played the leading role in the village administration.

2. Religious Transformation

The role of mission school in the religious aspect was of immense significance in the transitional period of the Mizo traditional belief to Christianity. The content of the textbook and the role played by the school teacher will be focused on this aspect.

School Education: Means for Religious Conversion

Literal meaning of conversion simply can mean the adoption of a new identity of religion or a change from one religious identity to another.

According to Frederick Downs, "In North East India as a whole and in particular Mizoram the same missions were often working with the same method as other part of India and the amount of money expended was never exceptionally large."[261] Interestingly, unlike the other region in India, the growth of Christianity was rapidly increased among the Mizo. In the study of mission school education, it is worthy to be recited from Frederick Downs how A.T Embree explained the importance of education to the 19th century evangelical:

> Their basic concept was the character of man [humankind] was a product, not of his [/her] physical, but of his [/her] moral environment, and that salvation could be achieved and the individual could be totally transformed by a direct assault on the mind. Education followed by personal conversion would change the whole nature of society.[262]

Frederick Downs rightly said that this understanding (A.T Embree's explanation of the importance of education) of the relationship between education and evangelism is understood in the explanation that the missionaries themselves gave for their deep participation in school work.[263] As too in Mizoram, the missionaries significantly used school education as one of the instruments for evangelization. The role of education in evangelization or conversion can be broadly divided into two functional aspects

First, the Mizo students were directly taught the Gospel by the missionaries in the school. Therefore, the school became the center for hearing the Gospel. It is evident from the report in

1913 by J.H. Lorrain saying: "Many of the boys in Mr. Savidge's boarding school have been concerted and several of them were baptized last week. Others are still under instruction in catechumen class."[264] This shows that the missionaries used the school as one of the centers for preaching the Gospel.

Second, to abandon the religiosity in terms of superstitions and taboos, some lessons were included in the "Lushai Premer" prepared by D.E. Jones and Pasena published in 1929, which encounter the superstition and the taboo in Mizo society. In the textbook, it was cleverly constructed to counteract by giving the heading "which are not fearful":

Sih;[265] *Zawngluro* (Gibbon's skull); *tuivamit*[266] (water spring a small pool of water); *lei chat* (crack in the earth); *thing lu bul* (a broken off tree), *tui lut* (a stream flows into a hole); *sarthi* (accidental death), *lei ruang tuam* (a mound resembling a grave), *chham ek* (a reddish deposit found at the bottom of some pools or where water has run)[267] In fact, all these things were taboos and superstitious, and feared by the Mizos in the olden days. In continuation of the above points of "Not Fearful," the following points are also included:

1. *Kawnah Ramhuai a liam bik lo* (the saddle of the hill is not haunted by malevolent spirit).[268]

2. *Lungpui leh Lunglianin huai an nei lo* (Huge rocks and big trees are not the home of evil).

3. *Keptuam*[269] *leh rulke nei hmu mah ila kan thi bik lovang* (No one will die of seeing *keptuam* and snake with leg).

4. *Thingsairua*[270] *nen, thingzungkai*[271] *nen, thinghlang*[272] *nen, fangfar*[273] *nen a hlauhawm lo. (Thingsairua, thingzungkai, thinghlang and fangfar* are not fearful).

5. *Khaw kang leh sakei seh awmni kham tur a ni lo, in sakpui leh feh sak a sawt zawk.* (It is no use to observe public holiday due to village fire or someone killed by tiger, but helping them to build houses and clearing jhum is far better).

6. *Sih*[274] *a hlauhawm lova, tui bawlhhlawh in erawh chu a tha lo* (*Sih* is not dangerous, but drinking dirty water is unhealthy).

7. *Lova in thawi hi engmah a sawt lova, hna thawk ila, Pathianin mal a sawm zawk ang.*(sacrifices at *jhum* is no use at all rather work harder and God will bless you).

This lesson had been learned more than 50 years before the edition of Lushai Primer, which was published in 1959.[275] These lessons gradually convinced the mind of the Mizos and later they almost abandoned their traditional taboos, which played vital roles in shaping the moral and ethical life, for they were interpreted as superstitions. Z.T. Sangkhuma rightly said that the textbook that we have learned during childhood significantly directed our belief and lifestyle.[276] Zairema also expresses the effect of this as follows:

> After we were Christianized, we taught ourselves to deride the traditional beliefs which have been observed with deep respect. We were taught not to be afraid of *sarthi, leiruang tuam, thinglu bul, tuivamit,* etc. that are useful to keep the community life secure such as not to build house obstructing the road or at the tributary of the spring, etc. These were all despised as superstitions without any substitutions from the Christian ethical teaching. This makes the Mizo community who fear neither God nor human beings.[277]

Education and evangelization could not be separated in the mission work in Mizoram. As mentioned earlier, during the period when education was under the responsibility of the mission, Scripture and Christian moral value occupied the center place in its contents. Therefore, in the conversion process in Mizo society, educational function cannot be ignored.

Second, it has already been pointed out in Chapter 1 and also on the above point that right from the beginning, the Mizos who learnt to read and write would go and teach their fellow Mizos as soon as they themselves had mastered it. They therefore played a very important role in the spread of education, and thereby creating a new awareness among the people. Apart from this, they also shared their new knowledge of the Gospel. As early as 1900, Jones was able to write in his report, "By this time some of the Lushais help us in our work, both in teaching and preaching."[278] Savidge also wrote in his report in 1916 saying, "We have now nine village schools [in the southern part of Mizoram] and the school masters usually conducts the Sunday and week-day services. As he is more advanced than the ordinary villager he is able to help them in many ways."[279] Therefore, those who received the Gospel directly from the missionaries passed on the Gospel to their fellow ones. This shows the significant role played by the native teachers in religious aspect.

The Role of the Native Teachers

The role of the native school teachers in religious aspect among the Mizos is reasonably remarkable. Focus will be given on the role of teachers in evangelization and church planting.

Evangelization

The role of the Native teachers toward the evangelization of the Mizo people is fairly impressive. They gave priority to evangelization and preaching of the Gospel over their educational responsibility and consider preaching and sharing the Gospel as the primary responsibility and duty of a school teacher.[280] It is also noteworthy that the scripture was included as one of the subjects taught in the schools.[281]

The native teachers also took charge of evangelization and church administration in the village whenever and wherever the village schools were started.[282] It was indeed the school teachers who preached the Gospel and brought many to Christ apart from these foreign missionaries and a few itinerant evangelists. It was through their education that they managed to win people for Christ. They would travel to distant places to preach the Good News to others at the end of the school term. Their enthusiasm toward evangelization soon paid off in 1901 resulting in the submission of the surrendered *kelmei*[283] to the missionaries as is seen in the report of Toka [Tawka], who was one of the first three Mizo teachers.[284]

In 1978, Zairema clearly asserts that "It is not possible to talk about the work in the Lushai hills without considering the contribution made by primary school teachers."[285] Mendus, describing his visit to villages on the Mizoram-Chin Hills border in 1939, also believed that the continuation of pagan superstitions in the region was due to the lack of sufficient schools and Christian teachers in the area. Later, he found out to his joy and surprise that there were many who were willing to become Christians if they had access to education since the mission stations were 9 or 10 days' journey away from these villages and that the pastor of their district could only pay them occasional visits. He also expressed his hope that a teacher would be placed there in the succeeding year.[286]

Although the missionaries introduced the Gospel, in fact, without the contribution made by the natives, the Gospel would not have prevailed among the Mizos. In fact, we cannot underestimate the value and contributions of the mission schools and the Mizos themselves in the evangelization of the Mizos. We would not be wrong in saying that many people became Christians because of the education they received in the schools.

Church Planting and Administration

During the early days of Christianity in Mizoram, the school teachers were also comprehensively involved in church planting within the villages. Consequently, wherever a church was established, naturally they act as the church leaders. The foreign missionaries then gave the teachers the status of Church elders and membership to the presbytery[287] and they served as Chairman, Secretary, Preacher, and Sunday School teacher in the churches. After the ordination of elders was introduced in 1910, most of the mission school teachers were ordained. Although a considerable number of teachers were not ordained, yet they were usually looked up to as leaders. Lalhmuaka thus comments, "We would not be wrong in saying that the Pastors and the Evangelists ministered the churches which the teachers have planted"[288] which makes clear the primary role of the mission teachers toward the foundation of the churches in Mizoram.

The mission schools highly encouraged the spread of the Gospel because the teachers, though some not formally ordained, shared the same enthusiasm with that of the pastors. Even in villages without Christians, the establishment of a school was soon followed by an increase in the amount of believers and subsequently a congregation soon grew in that village. This also implies that the mission schools greatly contributed to the growth of the church and the Christians' life in Mizo society. The role of the teachers was not limited only to formal education but also includes religious teachings as well. As Saiaithang rightly said that in the truest sense, they played multiple roles of a school teacher while being a preacher as well as an evangelist.[289]

From 1913 onward, in Mizoram, the ordination of pastor was practiced; however, engagement of the mission school teachers in the church administration did not change very much because the pastors were still a few in number to meet the need of a vast area of pastorates.[290] The pastors needed to spend most of their time traveling from one village to another, looking after different churches in different villages within one pastorate. They were responsible for a district of roughly 30–50 square miles, which demanded sometimes a day's journey through the forest between each village. Therefore, it is not possible for the pastors to confine in one church where they were residing. The mission teachers played a significant role to look after the churches and their position was somewhat like that of modern days of assistant pastors.[291] Admitting the significant role played by the teacher, the first presbytery meeting held in North Mizoram on April 22, 1910 at Aizawl, they decided to include the teachers as one of the members in the Presbytery.[292] Mendus further commented on their usefulness saying, thus, "The role of the teacher is a great help for the Church. If the mission can recruit and post a teacher in every village, it will be helpful for the Church development."[293]

As it has been discussed the role of mission school education, it can be learned that education played a significant role in transforming Mizo traditional culture. There is no denying the fact that mission school education and the Gospel made a great contribution to the progress of Mizo society. From the religious perspective, Mizoram can be called one of the fastest-growing churches in the world. All the Mizos were converted into Christianity within less than 60 years from the arrival of the missionaries.[294]

3. School Education as Means for Safeguard for Colonial Rule

There was a system of "forced labor" in Mizoram since the British occupied the hill areas, by which each household must supply one *coolie* (laborer) to work for at least 10 days per annum.[295] This is termed in Mizo language as *Kuli* and the Mizo took this job as a great burden. In some cases, there was a term and condition for the exemption of "forced-labor", which the Mizos termed as *Kuli Awl*, which simply means "exemption from forced-labor." The *Kuli awl* (exemption from forced labor) was also used as one of the means for the increase of enrollments of the student in the early period of education in Mizoram.

In 1905, Major Shakespeare made an order asking the people of the village to build their school building voluntarily without salary. Under the forced labor system, Shakespeare permitted 120-day labor to be credited to each village, which built a school building and 120-day labor for the school teacher's house, and 50-day labor for annual repairs. All the officers were instructed to take up the action and to appropriate record in the labor enroll.[296]

B. Lalthangliana and Lawmsanga also pointed out some imperial elements to be found in the Mizo Primer. The Duhlian Primer published in 1915 had initially aimed at abandoning the traditional beliefs, taboos, and the possession of the evil spirits, nomadic life and developing the moral and the social relationship.[297] Moreover, there was a compulsion to submission to the colonial power. Some of the maxims inculcate in the Primer (textbook) which are mentioned by Lawmsanga with some changes in English translation are recited as follows.[298]

Pem fo suh (Do not be nomadic).

Bawihah awm tha rawh (Be a faithful slave)

Dawi a awm lo (There is no magic)

Puakphur haw suh (Do not dislike forced labor)

Thlaichhiah a sawt lo (Offering things for spirit is worthless)

Hmei neih a tha lo (It is immoral to have a concubine)

Chhiahhlawh entleu suh (Do not look down on the servant)

Khawlaiah hrit en suh (Do not stay outside while searching lice)

Ruang zawng zawng phum tur a ni (All the corpses must be buried).

From the above some saying, it can be learned that some of the lessons inculcated within the textbook are to counteract some of the practices of the Mizo. For instance, Mizos were nomadic in primitive society, thus this nature subsequently affects the development of the mission in terms of attendant of the school as we had already discussed. Thus, the missionary inculcated the maxim to change the thought pattern of the social reality among the Mizo. Moreover, the sayings "do not dislike force labor," "be faithful slave" are to mold the Mizos to be obeyed the imperialistic practice by the government.

Although there are many constructive maxims, it is also evidenced from the new maxim inculcated in the textbook that the mission school education imparted an imperialist ideology within the hearts of the Mizos. As it had been discussed in the second chapter in the Mizo school textbook, Primer Book, they included like ...*the white people are the wisest and most powerful...* It is worthy to recite Lawmsanga quote Lalthangliana by translating Mizo version into English version It is surprising to put these manifestations of imperialist attitudes in the Mizo textbook. The lessons which were taught in the school and the Mizo society was influenced in this way for nearly 50 years with the aims of colonizing. The effect was really powerful and influential; it successfully inculcated the minds of the Mizos with the idea that the white people are the most superior till today.[299]

Thus, there are some evidence that the mission education was used for safeguarding the colonial rule. Moreover, one of the most noteworthy impacts of the mission school education on Mizo society is that the admiration of the white people is still present day.

4. Impact of Education on Mizo Society

From the foregoing discussion, it is evidenced that the role played by mission school is of great significance in the transformation of the traditional Mizo society. Now focus will be given to the impact of mission school education in wider aspects.

Unification of the Society

As it has been discussed in the second chapter, in traditional Mizo society, every Mizo village was an independent sovereign administration. There were different clans having different dialects. There are several communities that include *Lushais, Kukis, Himars, Paithes, Pang, Raltes*, and *Pawis*, which agglomerate to form more unity among them. Each of these tribes spoke a different dialect that was unique to its culture. A raid between village to village was also very common. C.L. Hminga said that there was no cohesive force or system to bind the villages together but Christianity unified them.[300] He quoted Mr Agarwal to justify his argument:

> Missionaries helped the tribal community acquire a due sense of unity centering around a common religion, and the gap was soon cemented by the common faith. The introduction of Roman as the common script and the same religious books and hymns written in different tribal dialects which everyone could read paved the way to solidarity, and became the most important factors of the new religion creating a new and integrated community. The days of 'Luseis' and other tribes were over, and the Mizo society was born(sic).[301]

The formation of the Mizo language into written form and the used Mizo language as a common language resulted in unity in society. H.S. Luaia also stated that Mizos are fortunate to have the common language while the Khasis and Nagas were having different dialects.[302] In fact, the use of Mizo language is one of the factors that bind together the Mizo community.

However, as mentioned earlier, what is known as *Mizo ṭawng* (Mizo language) is originally the *Duhlian* dialect, which was the dialect of the elite group of that day. Therefore, one must also not ignore how unjust it may have seemed be for the smaller clans, which had their own dialect.

Growth in the Literature

Soon after school education was introduced by the Christian mission, indigenous leaders stepped forward to introduce various kinds of literatures. The "*Mizo leh Vai chanchinbu*," which was said to be the first weekly journal, was started in the month of November 1902. At first, J. Shakespear and A. R. Giles looked after this journal till 1910 after which the Mizos took care of it. Makthanga became editor from 1911 to 1936 and he was succeeded by Lalkailuaia Sailo till it was discontinued in 1941.[303] The Christian monthly journal, "*Krista Tlangau*," was commenced from October 1911.[304] R. Dala became the first editor in which 300 copies were made at the beginning.

Besides these literatures, translated work has been done from some English books that were thought to be useful for their Christian life. "The Pilgrim's Progress" by John Bunyan was translated in Mizo by Challiana and Chuautera in 1908.[305] This had been used as the one of the textbooks during in middle section in 1980s. Subsequently, "The Story of the Bible" written by Charles Foster. Rev. Challiana and F. W. Savidge translated from English to Mizo, which was published in 1909. A historical book written by Rev. Liangkhaia "Mizo Chanchin" is worthy to be noted here to be regarded as a milestone in research work. This book was written as early as 1926 but the publication was only in 1938.[306] This book served as one of the important primary sources in writing the history of the Mizos.

Subsequently, many literary works came out of the Mizos and the number of books is available to be read in Mizo language. In this, the mission school education played an important role in the growth of literature in Mizo society. These literatures served as spiritual nourishment, giving instruction, challenge, and building relationship between churches that were established at different places to meet the need of their context. Moreover, they served as a source material for research work for the present days' researchers.

However, the forerunners of the literature work among the Mizos were greatly influenced by the western missionaries. Therefore, most of the literatures, in the area of history of Christianity and in its related aspects, all credit was given to the missionaries. This further had an impact on the earlier Mizo writers to be uncritical in analyzing the missionaries' work before 2000s. For instance, Rev. V.L Zawnga said though the missionaries might have made many mistakes he did not want to point out their mistake rather he was more comfortable to praise their valuable work.[307] However, in contemporary period, as a result of improvement in academic exercises and scholarship, which looked the Christian mission and their work in new perspective, new approaches have emerged in evaluating Christianity and it impacts in Mizoram in particular.

Refining of *Tlawmngaihna*

The writer agreed with C.L Hminga as he said that Christianity refines *Tlawmngaihna*.[308]

The moral conduct of Mizo which is known as *Tlawmngaihna* is continued among the Mizos. But one's performance to be a *Tlawmngai* (verb of *Tlawmngaihna*) person is simultaneously changed as the religious and social transformation takes place. After the transformation of the Mizo society in terms of religion and sociality, old and traditional requirements were not valued any more. For instance, in religious terms, the Mizo embraced Christianity; it was no more necessary to perform *Thangchhuah*, which demanded heroic acts, show of bravery, and expertise in hunting.

The changing context of the traditional Mizo society to modern society also needed to be considered in this aspect. In contemporary Mizo society due to improvement in infrastructure, the traditional practice of a *Tlawmngai* person was also no longer necessary. For instance, as a result, development in road communication and due to availability of motor vehicles, carrying sick people by the villagers from villages to villages is no more necessary. Hunting wild animal is also no more valued, raids between villages are also no more practiced, all these practices were the areas where the Mizo youth show their *Tlawmngaihna*.

Therefore, as a result of the continuation of the Christian moral values, which complement the Mizo mode of conduct called *Tlawmngaihna* still prevails among the Mizo. It is evident from the contribution made by the Mizo teachers, discussed earlier. However, *Tlawmngaihna* seems to be in decline because of modernization and development in different areas.

Thus, Mizo moral and ethical principle of *Tlawmngaihna* were redefined in the light of the Gospel eliminating its negative impact.[309] *Zawlbuk* (bachelor house), the place of learning of *Tlawmngaihna*, was abolished, but *Tlawmngaihna* survives in the Christian context in a redefined form because *Tlawmngaihna*, "self-sacrifice for others" and "doing good to others" remains in agreement with the Gospel. Therefore, *Zawlbuk* the Mizos traditional institution no longer survives, but the spirit of *Zawlbuk* known as *Tlawmngaihna* still survives in the hearts of the Mizos. As a result, in all the villages and towns, "Young Mizo Association (YMA)" a voluntary organization is formed in order to help people in various ways.

YMA as it is popularly known today was formerly called Young *Lushai* Association (YLA) when it was formed on June 15, 1935 by the Christian missionaries and the pioneer Mizo Christians. In spite of countless terrors and resistance against Christianity which found its roots in Mizoram in 1894, the entire region was swept by Christianity within a decade. Even the chiefs and their subordinates started to recognize and embrace it. Various churches and institutions came into existence resulting in the decline of the *Zawlbuk* (Bachelor's dormitory) which was one of the most esteemed establishments among the Mizos. While the number of participants in schools and churches increased, the attendance in *Zawlbuk* met a drastic fall. The attempt of the Governor to bring about revival in the *Zawlbuk* institution had no significant outcome. Thus, the most-valued institution came to a sad end. The Christian missionaries and church leaders found it necessary to establish an institution that could take the place of *Zawlbuk* now that it was gone. Consequently, a meeting was summoned at the residence of a Christian missionary Miss Katie Hughes (Pi Zaii) on June 3, 1935. "Young Mizo Kristian Association" was one of the names suggested but it was rejected due to its exclusive nature. One of the Christian missionaries Rev. David Edward (Zorema Pa) suggested that "YLA" would be most fitting and it was agreed that it would officially start functioning from June 15, 1935.[310]

It is therefore right to maintain the view that even in the postcolonial era, though no *Zawlbuk* institution can be seen, yet the spirit of *Zawlbuk* together with *Tlawmngaihna* is actively functioning within the Mizo community.

However, as mentioned earlier, moral conduct or *Tlawmngaihna* is not the priority in the contemporary Mizo cultural values. This does not mean that *Tlawmngaihna* is no more valued but it means that there are other things that are more valued by the Mizo. For instance, higher qualification in education is more valued in Mizo society. This is evidenced from the rapid growth of literacy rate in Mizoram.

Impact on the Mizo Women

One of the remarkable changes in Mizo society's traditional customs occurred in the status of women. In the traditional Mizo society, women had been mere possessions to be acquired, beaten, or disposed of at men's will. There is a significant impact in terms of education and Christianity in Mizoram that changed women's status for the better.

In the traditional Mizo society, there was no chance for the Mizo women to attend the *Zawlbuk* institution. By abolishing the *Zawlbuk* institution, and establishing mission schools, discrimination against women in the field of education has come to an end.[311] The following table shows the growth of the position of women in literacy since 1971–2001.

Table 3 Sex-wise literacy (in percentages) rates in Mizoram, 1971–2001[312]

Year	Male	Female
1971	60.49	46.71
1981	64.46	54.91
1991	85.65	78.60
2001	90.69	86.13

As a result of the growth of literacy rate, simultaneously, the number of educated women increased in Mizoram.

In contemporary, Mizo society, many women are engaged in government office, business, and political administration.[313]

In religious areas too as early as 1916, the Mizo women evangelists' team known as "Bible women" who were able to read the Bible was appointed by the mission to work for the uplift of the Mizo women. The reason for bearing the name "Bible Women," was that they carried the Holy Bible along with them.

According to the record of the report of the Lushai Hills 1903 by Rev. D.E Jones, there were three evangelists and one Bible women supported by the church. The report has not mentioned the name of the "Bible women" and her detailed work. Therefore, it is not known how long she continued her works. In 1916, the first batch of women workers was appointed, namely, Bualthluaii, Thangluuaii, Chhingtei of Aizawl, Chhingtei of Durtlang, and Dochhungi. After some time, more people were appointed. Altogether, they were 21 in number. Therefore, as a result of emergence of Mizo illiterate women, the women's ministry was also developed in Mizo society.[314] However, concerning the position of women in the churches in Mizoram, till today woman ordination is not fully supported by the Mizos. Only one woman was ordained by the BCM while the other churches do not yet ordain any women for pastor.[315]

Impact on Occupation

Traditionally, Mizos were engaged in jhum cultivation. As a result of the establishment of education in Mizoram, many people became capable of garnering a government job. Many too were engaged in business and industrial work. Thus traditional occupation was more and more changed by the modern system of occupation like industry, business, etc. However, the old method of jhuming cultivation cannot be yet stopped in Mizoram.

In 2010, like many other developing countries, almost 70% of the Mizo population is partially dependent on agriculture. But the production is far from self-sufficient due to lack of reliable methods of farming, lack of infrastructure and declining fertility of the topsoil. About 95% of Mizoram farmers are still practicing a century-old method of shifting cultivation contributing to severe soil depletion and environmental problems. It was found that 75000 rural families cleared 45 acres each of forests annually for food crop cultivation. Based on the Indian Council of Agricultural Research's calculation, the total topsoil loss because of shifting cultivation in Mizoram can be estimated to be around 1383750 tons annually.[316] It can be said that to educate the people on this aspect, education is not much successful among the Mizos.

The Rise of the Elite

As a result of the rapid growth in literacy and increase of educated people, soon education will be considered a requirement for salaried jobs and a welcome relief from the tiresome labor of hard work. McCall views that the mission school education was responsible for the emergence of a privileged class. He added, "black-coated occupations became synonymous with progress, and Christianity led towards black-coatism."[317] He further says, "It has beckoned the young Mizos towards distant lands and ideas rather than towards the uplift of their land of birth, the land of their future. The salaried post had been termed a 'dead end' because it often marked the cessation of all future real effort".[318] Therefore, MacCall rightly observed that the education system produced the privilege in which the Mizos' background had little in common. It is impressive to quote from Mac Call:

> From the start, it was only the children and relations of the 'new rich' for whom the new and novel experience of middle and higher became possible. Among the new rich, in addition to mission

workers, can be included the salaried employees of Government. In this way all through the years the salaried classes have retained their initial advantage, and it is their sons, daughters, and relatives, who have all along enjoyed advantages, not easily open to the ordinary and typical Lushai villager, whose resources for education, after the free primary course, could only be derived from the toilsome labour of producing surplus crops, and from still the more difficult task of converting this surplus into cash, within an economy that contained no provision for export or adequate marketing. It was in this way that kind of oligarchy or intelligential that has sprung up, which has no place in indigenous society of the Lushai.[319]

Western education provided and advantaged thus avenue for getting government jobs and also became the new locus of prestige comparable to the traditional elites and elders, decidedly as the educated were free from manual labor and from jhum fields. As C. Nunthara has said that they enjoy a kind of life hitherto considered to be the monopoly of the British people.[320] Government jobs provided cash to the incumbents. With the introduction of cash economy and the relatively low level of agriculture production, especially cash crops as almost all the agriculture products were for home consumption, it became an important criterion for attaining prestigious position among the people. As such parents planned the future of their children in such a way that they would get a prominent position, removing them from the burden of jhum cultivation, through education.[321]

Therefore, the mission school educated people who either worked with the churches or government employees and received payment in cash were the forerunners in doing petty business, building up the benefits of monetary transactions.[322] In this way, a division began to take shape between traditional elites and the emerging new middle class. The new elite class was the offspring of the mission school and largely allied to the churches.

Therefore, though the mission school education was the means for upward mobility of the Mizo, it also created the emergence of an elite group in Mizo society. The educated people had more opportunities to get jobs, which further resulted better condition in livelihood. It was in this way that a kind of oligarchy or intelligentsia emerged that had no place in the indigenous society of the Mizos.

Conclusion

After the establishment of formal education in Mizoram, there was a transformation of the intellectual among the Mizo. The role of the native teacher with *Tlawmngaihna* was immensely significant. The native teachers were the foundation in reshaping the village leaders in Mizoram.

In religious aspect, the transformation of the traditional belief of the Mizo into Christian faith, the school textbook and the role of native teachers are important factors. To counter the act of superstitious and taboo, some lessons were prepared in the textbook. However, the mission school through the lessons in the textbook was also used as a means for safeguard for colonial rule or a means for justifying the colonial rule. For instance, the forced labor was justified through a lesson in the textbook teaching the student, "it must be not opposed." The impact of the mission school education can be varied. Some significant impacts are:

First, it unified different clans of the Mizo society by introducing the Mizo language as a common language. However, what is called *Mizo ṭawng* (Mizo language) is the *Duhlian* dialect, the language of elite group of those days. Therefore, one must not ignore how painful it would have been for other clans when one particular dialect was prominent over others.

Second, it uplifted the status of women in Mizo society. Women in the traditional Mizo society were voiceless and dominated by menfolk. It was uplifted by education in many aspects. However, its implications were controversial. For example, the patriarchal nature of the Mizo society is not the only responsible factor for the lack of women's ordination, as the absence of missionary effort in pursuing in that line as well.

Third, to some extent, Mizo traditional occupation of jhum cultivation was changed into business, industries, government jobs, etc. It can be said that education is failed in abandoning the old system of cultivation as many as about 70% of the total population is still engaged in jhum cultivation, which resulted in deforestation.

Fourth, in terms of *Tlawmngaihna*, the moral values of the traditional Mizo society were also refined by Christian teaching. For instance, it was no longer necessary to be a *Tlawmngai* person to attain *Thangchhuah* title as was of no has value in the context Mizo Christians. However, it seems that the value of *Tlawmngaihna* in Mizo society has been replaced by the educational values and the modernity.

Finally, the emergence of the elite groups was also due to the impact of mission school education. There were people who got the benefit and privilege through mission school education. This further resulted in gaps in the society between the privileged class and the other.

Conclusion

In the traditional Mizo society, the Mizos did not have a written script. In spite of the absence of the written script, the Mizos had a set of their norms for moral conduct and for the welfare of their community. One of the binding factors in the traditional Mizo society was informal education. The sociocultural and religious values were imparted through their informal education in which *Zawlbuk* was a valuable institution for the Mizos. However, *Zawlbuk* education was limited to young men and boys, whereas women and girls were not allowed to enter *Zawlbuk*. Thus, the family was the only educational institution for the female members of the Mizo society. In spite of the limitation of women's education, they were well trained by their parents to take responsibility for their family.

The moral code of conduct which in Mizo term *Tlawmngaihna* occupied the center of the Mizo informal education. The aspect of *Tlawmngaihna* covered a wide range. It covered the whole notion of the sociocultural and political life of the traditional Mizo society. For instance, in religious terms, the most valued aspect was to perform Thangchhuah, which was considered as the passport to paradise. The social life in which raids between villages happened were considered as preparing the Mizo youth to be brave and heroic. To perform all these moral and ethical code of conduct, *Tlawmngaihna* was the guiding principle in the Mizo society.

In spite of a formal education system, the traditional Mizo society was bound by an informal moral system, which has based on awards, for bravery and heroic acts; proverbial sayings that exhorted the people to be morally and ethically discerning to build a strong sociocultural society. This tradition was impacted by the values and norms that came along with the advent of the British, the missionaries and their formal education system, which was largely built on a written script, formal school, etc.

The introduction of formal education by the missionaries, through the use of Mizo language as a medium of instruction in school, resulted that the *Duhlian* language to become a common language among the Mizo, which became an important factor for the unity of Mizo society. However, it is important to look at whether the minority clan who are using different dialects willingly accepted this process of change or not. The development of the Mizo language and its impact would be an interesting subject for further research, as in this book, deep analysis is not done in this area. Although the missionaries initiated the native language as a medium of instruction, English was also introduced as a medium of instruction after a short period of time, since the introduction of mission school education. The introduction of English as one of the means of instruction in the school is considered as an effective tool for colonization.

After the introduction of formal school, the growth of literacy rate was rapidly increased among the Mizos. This resulted in the transformation of the intellect level among the Mizos. In fact, missionaries were the initiators concerning education and evangelism; however, without the contribution and the effort made by the indigenous teachers, the development of education, and the rapid growth of literacy rate would not have happened as it was.

Another remarkable role and impact played by the mission school education was in empowering the status of Mizo women. As a result of the establishment of education, women were uplifted in Mizo society. In the secular realm too, women held a high level of government jobs and reached up to the highest level in some offices in Mizoram as well as abroad.

The impact of education on the growth of Mizo literature is also worthy to be noted. As a result of the effort made by the earlier Mizo educated people, the Mizo literature remains an important resource of the Mizo social religious life. The forerunners of the literature work were greatly influenced by the western missionaries. Therefore, most of the literatures in the area of history of Christianity and its related aspects remain colonized missionaries. The credit goes to the missionaries for encouraging intellectual genre of writing. This further had an impact on the earlier Mizo writers to be uncritical of the missionaries and their mission. However, in contemporary period, as a result of the improvement in academic exercises and scholarship, new approaches have been made in evaluating Christianity and its impact on Mizoram.

The study also discovered that the mission education provided an opportunity for getting government jobs and entering in trade business. This further resulted in the emergence of a privileged group among the Mizos. Government jobs provided cash to the incumbents. With the introduction of cash economy and the relatively low level of agriculture production, especially cash crops as almost all the agriculture products were for home consumption, it became an important criterion for attaining respected position among the people. Therefore, the mission school educated people who either worked in the churches or in the government received payment in cash, and thus were the forerunners in doing petty business and building up the benefit of the monetary transactions. This resulted in the emergence of the privileged group in Mizo society.

As mission school education was introduced, structural changes in sociopolitical aspect of the Mizo traditional society could be discovered. The role and function played by Elders and *Val Upa,* who were older in terms of ages, were given a great value and respect in the traditional Mizo society and were replaced by the educated people. The influential role played by the *Val Upa* and the elders as adviser under Mizo chiefs' administration was sidelined by the educated people. The intellectual people who were capable as teachers became more influential in the villages. The teacher became a prominent figure in Mizo society. The role of the teachers was not only limited to formal education but also as a religious teacher, as a preacher as well as an evangelist.

Mission school education was also used as a means to justify the colonial rule in Mizoram. For justification of the practice of the forced labor by the government, which was considered as a heavy burden by the Mizos, lessons in the textbooks are also imparted. In reverse, the exemption of forced labor to the parent of the boy student, which was granted at the request of the missionaries, also revealed the intervention of the colonial power in the development of mission school education. Therefore, it can be said that the British administrators imposed changes and the missionaries convinced the people by telling the necessity of such transformations.

However, it also exposed that in certain cases, the British administrators and the missionaries had different views and sometimes clashed over in different aspects. For example, while the missionaries made an effort to establish high school in Mizoram but the government officials reluctant to give permission. However, it was started late in 1944 as a high demand and contribution made by the indigenous people. Therefore, for further research, the issues with regard to "the government policy and the Christian mission in Mizoram" will be an interesting topic that has not been touched deeply in this book.

In responding to the research questions, the study also reveals that these western values were also imparted through the textbooks and curriculum. Colonial ideas were also imparted through education to the Mizo bringing in an inferiority complex among the natives. For instance, there were discrepancies in the textbook published by the missionaries in which the white European race was alleged to be superior, loyalty to the government than any other races. Furthermore, English language, western songs, names of the months, etc. were introduced as replacement of indigenous culture. Wrestling, one of the most common and valued of the traditional games, was abandon as we did not find any attempt to revive and to continue in the school curriculum.

It is evident that the style of Mizo Christian song and music is greatly influenced by the western music. The traditional Mizo song tune was treated as unworthy or not holy enough to be sung inside the Church setting for a long period of time. Many local church leaders were not able to accept singing the Mizo traditional tune in the worship service. Later, a new type of tune that is neither western style nor Mizo traditional tune call *Lengkhawm zaithluk* was developed among the Mizo

Christians during the rival period and it is commonly sung in the worship service in every church till today. However, the pure Mizo traditional tuned *(Cheih lam Thuk)* song is hardly accepted by the present church elders to be sung in the worship service. Consequently, this has become one of the stumbling blocks in developing Christian songs with Mizo traditional tune. Traditional music and culture tell the historical past, where they come from and identity of people. It is an important part of the society's identification. This could be one of the regretful limitations made by the early missionaries and the first-generation Christians to Mizo society. As instead of encouraging people to embrace their culture and traditional Mizo tunes in a more Christian way, and praise God with their traditional music; they focused instead on changing the whole system by introducing the western style of music in the mission school education and making that as the only acceptable worthy music to be played in church.

Customs and ceremonies like sacrificial feast performed by the Mizo to get *Thangchhuah* title were totally abandoned. Drinking beer, which was a common social habit, was considered as unchristian. Therefore, theologically speaking, the understanding of the concept of sin was also changing. There are many changes in the traditional value system to the western value system. The traditional institution of *Zawlbuk*, where young men and children were trained in various aspects, was totally abandoned by the Mizos within a short period, since the establishment of formal education. As a result of analyzing the content and curriculum, many western value systems were imparted to the Mizo students through textbooks and system of education.

ॐ

Bibliography

PRIMARY SOURCES

Interview Thanchungnunga, K. BCM Pastor Pensioner, Aizawl. Interview, 16th September, 2010.

Sawiluaia. BCM Pastor Pensioner, Serkawn. Interview, 7th September, 2010.

Zawnga, V.L. BCM Pastor Pensioner, Aizawl. Interview, 15th September, 2010.

Reports *The Annual Reports of BMS on Mizoram 1901-1938.* Serkawn: Mizoram Gospel Centenary Committee, BCM, 1993.

Lalchawimawia, comp. *British Rule in Mizoram (collection of Important Documents Vol I,*

Missionary and the Government. n.p: Published by the Author, 2010.

Thanzauva, K., comp. *Reports of the Foreign Mission of the Presbyterian church of Wales on Mizoram 1894-1985.* Aizawl: The Synod Literature and Publication Boards, 1997.

School Textbooks Jones, D.E. *Duhlian Zirtirh Bu [Duhlian Primer].* Madras [sic]: SPCK Press, 1921, 5th edition.

Jones, D.E. and Pasena. *Zirtirh Bu Thar[New Primer].* Aijal [sic]: Loch Press, 1951, 26th edition.

___________ *Zirtirh Bu.* Aizawl: Synod Book Room, 1977, 10th edition.

Pasena. *Zirtirh Bu.* Shillong: Assam Authority, 1899.

Pasena. *Zirtirh Bu.* Aijal: The Wales Presbyterian Mission, 1929.

Rowland, Edwin. and Pasena. *Zirtirh Bu.* Aizawl: Loch Press, 1951, 26th edition.

Rowland, Edwin. *Bu Lai II-na [Middle Reader II].* Madras [sic]: SPCK, 1909.

Letters Aizawl Record File, No. 25684 dt. 27.3.1903. Letter from the D.P.I Assam to the Superintendent of Lushai Hills.

Aizawl Record File, No. 548 DC. Letter from M. Bradshaw Esqr, Sub-Divisional Officer, Lungleh to the Superintendent, Lushai Hills, Aizawl. Dated the 30th September 1913.

Order passed on Mr. Lorrain's letter dated the 13rd September, 1913 by the Superintendent, Lushai Hills. Memo. No. Dated Aijal. Dated the 20th October 1913.

Journal *Kristian Tlangau,* [Monthly Journal] (Aizawl: August, 1916).

Mizo leh Vai Chanchin bu [Monthly Journal] (n.p. February,1903).

Daily News Paper*Vanglaini* (Aizawl), 1st Sept. 2010.

Others Record Log book of Buanga [J.H. Lorrain's Diary book], Dated 26th October, 1894. BCM

Archives, Serkawn.

Mission Schools Exam Result Record Book. BCM Archives, Serkawn.

Presbyterian Church in Mizoram, Conference. Minute of the Meeting of the Presbytery, Aijal, April 22/1910. Aizawl Theological College Archives, Aizawl.

Books Allen, B.C. *Gazetteers of Bengal and North East India.* New Delhi: Mittal Publications, 1979.

Anderson, H. *Among the Lushais.* Calcutta: Carey Press, 1914.

Challiana. *Pi Pu Nun [the life of ancestors].* Aizawl: Trio Book House, reprint 1978.

Chapman E. and M. Clark. *Mizo Miracle.* Edited by Marjories Skyes. Madrass: Christian Literature Society, 1968.

Chatterji, N. *The Earlier Mizo Society.* Kolkata: Firma KLM Private Limited on behalf of Tribal Research Institute Department of Art and Culture Gov't. of Mizoram; Aizawl, 1975.

_____________ *Zawlbuk as a Social Institution in the Mizo Society.* Aizawl: Published by the Author, 1975.

Chatterji, N. The *Earlier Mizo Society.* Kolkata: Firma KLM Private Limited, on Behalf Tribal Research Institute, Department of Art & Culture, Gov't. of Mizoram, 1975.

Luaia, H.S. *Hmanlai Mizo Khawsak dan leh Mizoram Buai lai thu [Mizo Traditional Way of Life of and the Period of Insurgency in Mizoram].* Serkawn, Lunglei: H. Lalzoliana, 2004.

Luaia, *Mizo Nun Phung [The Life style of the Mizos].* Aizawl: Lal Riliani, 1998.

Lewin, T.H. *A Fly on the Wheel or How I helped to Govern India*. Aizawl: Tribal Research Institute, Department of Art & Culture, Gov't. of Mizoram, 1949, 3rd reprint, 2005.

Lorrain, J.H. *Dictionary of the Lushai Language*. Calcutta: Asiatic Society, 2nd reprint 1982.

Mc Call, A. G. *The Lushai Chrysallis*. Aizawl: Tribal Research Institute, Department of Art & Culture, Gov't. of Mizoram, 1949, 3rd reprint, 2003.

Mendus, E. Lewis. *The Diary of Jungle Missionaries*. Aizawl : The Synod Publication

Board, reprint 1984 of the original publication Liverpool: Foreign Mission Office Presbyterian Church of Wales, 1956.

Parry, N.E. *A Monograph On Lushai Customs & Ceremonies*. Calcutta: Firma KLM

Private Limited, 1928, 3rd reprint, 2009.

Reid, A.S. *Chin-Lushai Land*. Aizawl: Firma Private Limited for Tribal Research Institute

Government of Mizoram, 1893, reprint 2008.

SECONDARY SOURCES

Books Dharmaraj, Jacob. *Colonialism and the Christian Mission:Postcolonial Reflection*. Delhi: ISPCK, 1993.

Dawngliana, M.S. "Ministry of BCM Relief & Development Department," *BCM Conpendium* . Serkawn, Lunglei: Centenary Committee BCM, 2003.

Downs, Frederick S. "Christian Conversion Movements among the Hills tribe of North East India in the Nineteenth and Twentieth Centuries," in *Religion in South Asia*. Edited by G.A. Oddie. New Delhi: Manahor Publication, Second revised edition 1991. 155-174.

Downs, Frederick S. *History of Christianity in North East India,* Volume V, part 5. Bangalore: The Church History Association of India, 2003.

Grovers, Dorothy. *Set on a Hill: The Record of the Fifty Years in the Lushai Country.*

Compiled by the Gospel Centenary Committee, Baptist Church Of Mizoram, 1993.

Hawla, V. *Zoram Hmar Chan Zosapte Chanchin [The story of Missionaries of the*

Northern Mizoram]. Aizawl: The Synod Bookroom, 1969.

Hluna, J.V. *Education and Missionaries in Mizoram*. Guwahati: Spectrum Publications, 1992.

Hminga, C.L. *Life and Witness of the Churches in Mizoram*. Serkawn, Mizoram: The Literature Committee, Baptist Church of Mizoram, 1987.

Kane, J. Herbert. *Understanding Christian Mission*. Grand Rapids: Baker Book House, 1974.

Kipgen, Mangkhosat. *Christianity and Mizo Culture*. Aizawl: Mizo Theological Conference, 1997.

Khuanga. "The Role of Christianity in the Socio-Economic Praxis of Mizoram," *Toward a Tribal Theology: The Mizo Perspective*. Edited by K.Thanzauva, Aizawl, Mizoram: Mizo Theological Conference, 1989.

Lalbiakliana. *Mizoram Zirna Chanchin[The Story of Education in Mizoram]*. Aizawl: Education Department, Mizoram, 1979.

Lalchhinga. *Mizo Kristian Kohhran; A Chanchin hmasa lam leh Presbytery neih Hnulamte 1894-1939 [Mizo Christian Church: The story of the Beginning and After The formation of Presbyterian 1894-1930]*. Aizawl: L.M. Press, 1996.

Lalhmuaka, P.C. *Zoram Thim ata Engah [Zoram: From Darkness to Light]*. Aizawl: The Synod Publication Board, 1988.

Lalhmuaka. *Kristian Hmasate Tihduhdahna[The Early Christian [Mizo] Persecution]*. Aizawl: Synod Publication Board, 1991.

Lalhmuaka. *Zoram Zirna Lam Chhinchhiahna [The Records of Zoram Education]*. Aizawl: Tribal Research Institute, 1981.

Lalnghinglova. *Zoram ngahchhan [The Foundation of Mizoram]*. Aizawl:Saikungi, 1993.

Lalthangliana, B. *History and Culture of Mizo in India, Burma and Bangladesh*. Aizawl: Remkungi, 2001.

Lalthangliana, B. *Mizo Literature*. Aizawl: M.C. Lalrinthanga, second edition, 2004.

Lloyd, J. Meirion. *History of the Church in Mizoram: Harvest in the Hills*. Aizawl: Synod Publication Board, 1991.

Malsawma H.L *Sociology of the Mizos*. Guwahati: Spectrum Publications, 2002.

Nuthara, C. *Mizoram: Society and Polity*. Delhi: Indus Publishing Company, 1996.

Pandey, Ram Shakal. *Principles of Education*. Agra: Vinod Pustak Mandir, 1979.

Pieres, Aloysius. "Towards an Asian Theology of Liberation," in *Asia's Struggle for Full*

Humanity. Edited by Virginia Fabella, New York: Orbis, 1980.

Pudaite, Rochunga. *The Education of the Hmar People.* Sielmat: Indo-Burma Pioneer Mission, 1963.

Ralte, Lalhruaitluanga. *Zoram Vartian [The Early Dawn of the Zoram].* Aizawl: Fine Print, 2008.

Rokhuma, R.L. *Mizoram Zirna a Mission leh Kohhran Rawngbawlna [Mission and the Church Ministry Towards Mizoram Education].* Lunglei: Communication Department BCM, 1988.

Ryngnga. *The Life and Work of Revd William Williams.* Aizawl: Synod Publication Board, 1994.

Saiaithanga. *Mizo Kohhran Chanchin[The account of the Mizo Church].* Mizo District, Assam: The Regional Theological Literature Committee, 1969.

Sangkima. *Essay on Mizo History.* Guwahati: Spectrum Publication, 2004.

Shakespeare, John. *The Lushai-Kuki Clans,* Part-I. Aizawl: Tribal Research Institute, 1975.

Sugirtharajah, R.S. Ed., *Voices from the Margin Interpreting the Bible in the Third*

World. New York: Orbis/SPCK, New edition, second impression, 1997.

Thanga, Lal Biak. *The Mizos A Study in Racial Personality.* Guwahati: United Publisher. 1978.

Thanzauva, K. "Theology of Zawlbuk," *Towards a Tribal Theology: The Mizo Perspective.* Jorhat: The Mizo Theological Conference, 1989.

Vanlawma, C. *Tun Kum za Chhunga Mizo Hnam puipate 1894-1994[Outstanding Figures Among the Mizos Within this Century 1894-1994].* Aizawl: M.C. Lalrinthanga, 1994.

Verghese C.G. and R.L. Thanzawna, *A History of the Mizos.* vol. i. Delhi:Vikas Publishing House, 1997.

Woodthorpe, R.G. *The Lushai Expedition 1871-72.* Guwahati: Spectrum Publications, 1980.

Zairema, *God's Miracle in Mizoram.* Aizawl: Synod Press and Bookroom, 1978.

Zawla, K. *Mizo Pipute leh an Thlahte Chanchin[The Story of Mizo Ancestors and Their Decedents].* Aizawl: K. Zawla through the modern Printing Press, 1964.

Zairema, *Kan Bible* Hi *[Our Bible]*. Kolkata: Swapna Printing Works (P) Ltd., 2003.

DictionariesNeils, et al. *Concise Dictionary of the Christian World Mission.* Nashville: Abingdon Press, 1971.

Stuckard, Kankuvon. Ed., "Conversion," in *The Brill Dictionary of Religion Vol. I.*

Leiden, Boston: Brill, 2006.

Unpublished Materials Chawngthanpari. "*A Historical Study of the Educational Ministry of the Baptist Church of Mizoram since 1950s.*" Doctoral Thesis, Mysore University, 2006.

Lawmsanga. "*A Critical Study on Christian Mission with Special Reference To Presbyterian Church of Mizoram.*" D.Th. dissertation, University Birmingham Department of Theology and Religion, 2010.

Ngursangzeli, Marina. "*The role of The Early Mizo Mission School Teachers' Role in Witnessing to Christ.*" A paper presented at the CMS (Centre for

Mission Studies), Consultation on "Witnessing to Christ in Diverse Contexts," at the Union Biblical Seminary, Pune, Jan 12-14, 2010.

Rinchamliana. "*The History of the Mizo Bible Translation From 1897 to 1956: A Postcolonial Appraisal.*" M.Th. Thesis, Senate of Serampore College (University), 2010.

Journals and Periodicals Ralte, Lalrinawmi. "Dance Theology." *Journal of Asian Women's Resources Centre for Culture and Theology* 19/4 (December, 2000):35-39.

WebsitesLalthansangi. "A Situational Analysis of Women in Mizoram," A research report submitted to National Commission for Women, New Delhi. http://ncw.nic.in/pdfreports/Gender 20Profile-Mizoram. pdf. (6th Feb 2011).

Suantak, Vumson. "*Common Language for Zo(Chin) People in Burma*". http://zogamnuam.com. (17th Feb 2010).

"Proflie of YMA." An Officail website of Young Mizo Association. http://centralyma.org.in. (3rd March 2011).

"The Romanization of Toponyms in the Countries of South Asia." United Nations Group of Experts on Geographical Names Meeting of the Working Group on Romanization Systems Tallinn, 9-11 October 2006. *http://www.eki.ee/wgrs/wgr06_5.htm.* (21st Feb 2011).

ॐॐ

Endnotes

[1] K. Thanzauva, comp., "The report of the Lushai Hills, 1894," in *Reports of the Foreign Mission of the Presbyterian church of Wales on Mizoram 1894-1985* (Aizawl: The Synod Literature and Publication Boards, 1997), 1. C.L. Hminga, *Life and Witnesses of the Churches in Mizoram* (Serkawn: The Literature Committee, Baptist Church of Mizoram), 1987. 53-55. J. Herbert Lorrain and F.W. Savidge, "Report for 1903," in *The Annual Report on BMS on Mizoram 1901-1938* (Serkawn: Mizoram Gospel Centenary Committee, BCM, 1993), 6-7.

[2] For more detailed information of the social, cultural, and religious of the Mizo, see N.Chatterji, *The Earlier Mizo Society* (Kolkota: Firma KLM Limited, 1975, 2nd Reprint 2008); Lal Biak thanga, *The Mizos A Study in Racial Personality* (Guwahati: United Publisher, 1978); C.L. Hminga, *Life and Witness of the Churches in Mizoram* (Serkawn, Mizoram: The Literature Committee, Baptist Church of Mizoram, 1987); Mangkhosat Kipgen, *Christianity and Mizo Culture* (Aizawl: Mizo Theological Conference, 1997); Malsawma, *Sociology of the Mizos* (Guwahati: Spectrum Publications, 2002); B. Lalthangliana, *History and Culture of Mizo in India, Burma and Bangladesh* (Aizawl: Remkungi, 2001).

[3] Mangkhosat Kipgen, *Christianity and Mizo Culture* (Aizawl: Mizo Theological Conference, 1997), 63.

[4] J.H. Lorrain, *Dictionary of the Lushai Language* (Calcutta: Asiatic Society, 2nd reprint 1982), 562.

[5] N. Chatterji, *Zawlbuk as a Social Institution in the Mizo Society* (Kolkata: Firma KLM Private Limited, on behalf Tribal Research Institute, Department of Art and Culture, Gov't. of Mizoram, 1975), 61.

[6] N.E. Parry, *A Monograph on Lushai Customs & Ceremonies* (Calcutta: Firma KLM Private Limited, 1928, reprint 2009), 8.

[7] J.V. Hluna, *Education and Missionaries in Mizoram* (Guwahati: Spectrum Publications, 1992), 9.

[8] K. Zawla, *Mizo Pipute leh an Thlahte Chanchin [The Story of Mizo Ancestors and Their Decedents]*. Aizawl: K. Zawla through the modern Printing Press, 1964), 7.

[9] Lal Biak Thanga, *The Mizos* (Guwahati: United Publisher, 1978), 12.

[10] Malsawma, *Sociology of the Mizos* (Guwahati: Spectrum Publications, 2002), 55.

[11] Mangkhosat Kipgen, op.cit., 63.

[12] H. Anderson, *Among the Lushais*(Calcutta: Carey Press, 1914)**, 34**

[13] N.E. Parry, op.cit., 8.

[14] N.Chatterji, op.cit., 3.

[15] H.S. Luaia, *Hmanlai Mizo Khawsak dan leh Mizoram Buai lai thu* [*Mizo Traditional Way of Life of and the period of Insurgency in Mizoram]* (Serkawn, Lunglei: H. Lalzoliana, 2004), 3.

[16] Pu Buanga [J.L. Lorrain], *Log Book* [Personal diary book], BCM Archives, Serkawn.

[17] Mangkhosat Kipgen, op.cit., 63.

[18] *Ibid.*

[19] N. Chatterji, op.cit., 10.

[20] K. Thanzauva, "Theology of *Zawlbuk*," *Towards a Tribal Theology: The Mizo Perspective* (Jorhat: the Mizo Theological Conference, 1989),100.

[21] N.E. Parry,op.cit., 9.

[22] A.G. Mc Call, *The Lushai Chrysalis* (Aizawl: Tribal research Institute, 1949, 3rd reprint 2003), 191.

[23] H.S. Luaia, *Hmanlai Mizo Khawsak dan...*, op.cit., 6.

[24] N.E. Parry, op.cit., 11.

[25] N. Chatterji, *The Earlier Mizo Society* (Kolkata: Firma KLM Private Limited on behalf of Tribal Research Institute Department of Art and Culture, Gov't. of Mizoram; Aizawl, 1975), 76.

[26] *Val Upa* means an oldest young man, or the leader among the young men who are older in age.

[27] J.V. Hluna, *Education and Missionaries in Mizoram* (Guwahati: Spectrum Publications, 1992), 12.

[28] N. Chatterji, *Zawlbuk as a Social Institution...*,op.cit., 11.

[29] N.E. Parry, op.cit., 11.

[30] See K. Thanzauva, "Theology of *Zawlbuk*...", op.cit., 103-104.

[31] K. Thanzauva, "Theology of *Zawlbuk*...", op.cit., 104.

[32] N.Chatterji, *The Earlier Mizo Society...*, op.cit., 76-77.

[33] N.Chatterji, *The Earlier Mizo Society...*,op.cit, 76.

[34] N.E. Parry, op.cit.,9.

[35] *Ibid.*

[36] *Ibid.*,77.

[37] H.S. Luaia, *Hmanlai Mizo Khawsak dan...*, op.cit., 6.

[38] N. Chatterji, *The Earlier Mizo Society...*,op.cit.,76-77.

[39] J. Merion LLoyd, *History of the Church in Mizoram* (Aizawl: Synod Publication Board, 1991), 278.

[40] *Ibid.*

[41] K. Thanzauva, "Theology of *Zawlbuk*"..., op.cit., 102.

[42] N. Chatterji, *The Earlier Mizo Society...*, op.cit., 62.

[43] Ram Shakal Pandey, *Principles of Education* (Agra: Vinod Pustak Mandir, 1979), 27.

[44] John Shakespeare, *The Lushai-Kuki Clans, Part-I* (Aizawl: Tribal Research Institute, 1975), 16.

[45] Sangkima, *Essay on Mizo History* (Guwahati: Spectrum Publication, 2004), 146.

[46] C.L. Hminga, *Life and Witness...*, op.cit., 28.

[47] Sangkima, *Essay on Mizo History* (Guwahati: Spectrum Publication, 2004), 146.

[48] N.E. Parry, op.cit., 19.

[49] *Ibid.*

[50] *Ibid.*

[51] *Ibid.*

[52] All the seven points are cited from J.H. Lorrain, *Dictionary...*, op.cit., 513.

[53] H.L. Malsawma, op.cit., 63.

[54] Mangkhosat Kipgen, op.cit, 64.

[55] See, Khuanga, "The Role of Christianity in the Socio-Economis Praxis of Mizoram," *Toward a Tribal Theology: The Mizo Perspective*, edited by K.Thanzauva (Aizawl: Mizo Theological Conference, 1989), 96-98.

[56] See H. Lalmalsawma, op.cit., 64.

[57] A. G. Mc Call, op.cit., 182.

[58] A. G. Mc Call, op.cit., 182.

[59] A. G. Mc Call, op.cit., 182

[60] A. G. Mc Call, op.cit., 182.

[61] A.G. Mc Call, op.cit., 67.

[62] E. Chapman and M.Clark, *Mizo Miracle*, edited by Marjories Skyes (Madrass: Christian literature Society, 1968), 11.

[63] Cited by C.L. Hminga, *The Life and witness...*, op.cit.,32.

[64] There were two types of priests in traditional Mizo society: Priest who performed in traditional religious ceremonies for *Thangchhuah* and other religious ceremonies. He was responsible for invoking the blessing from God, they were called *Sadawt*. Another Priest was called *Bawlpu* who performed the rituals to propitiate the evil spirits to cure sickness.

[65] C.L. Hminga, *Life and Witness...*, op.cit., 34-36.

[66] *Ibid.*

[67] Challiana, *Pi Pu Nun [the life of ancestors]* (Aizawl: Trio Book House, Reprint 1978.) 54-56.

⁶⁸ *Thangchhuah Puan* is the name of a cloth worn as a mark of distinction by one who had coveted title of *Thangchhuah*, the wife and children of such a man are also entitled to wear this cloth. James Herbert Lorrain, *Dictionary of The Lushai Language…*, op.cit., 447.

⁶⁹ J.V. hluna, op.cit., 18.

⁷⁰ K. Thanzauva, *Theology of community: Tribal Theology in the Making* (Bangaloe: Asian Trading Corporation, 2004), 159.

⁷¹ For more detail of the story of Taitesena See K. Zawla, *Mizo Pipute leh an Thlahte Chanchin* (Aizawl: K. Zawla through the modern Printing Press, 1964), 248-254.

⁷² Challiana, Pipu Nun…,op.cit., 18. See also" Mangkhosat Kipgen, op.cit, 71.

⁷³ Dorothy Grovers, *Set On a Hill:The Record of the Fifty Years in the Lushai Country* (Serkawn The Gospel Centenary Committee, Baptist Church Of Mizoram 1993), 5.

⁷⁴ Cited by Mangkhosat Kipgen, op.cit., 17.

⁷⁵ Mangkhosat Kipgen, op.cit, 83.

⁷⁶ Mangkhosat Kipgen, op.cit, 87.

⁷⁷ For more detailed information of these heroes, see, K. Zawla, *Mizo Pipute leh…,*op. cit., 240-264.

⁷⁸ A.G. Mc Call, op.cit., 94.

⁷⁹ Chawngthanpari, "*A Historical Study of the Educational Ministry of the Baptist Church of Mizoram since 1950s,*" (Doctoral Thesis, Mysore University, 2006), 63.

⁸⁰ H.L. Malsawma, op.cit., 211. Also see K. Zawla, op.cit., 124.

⁸¹ Luaia, *Mizo Nun Phung [The Life style of the Mizos]* (Aizawl: Lal Riliani, 1998), 22.

⁸² The *Sial* is a large animal that is a high-valued domesticated animal among the Mizo, one of the indicators of a person's wealth was the number of Sial he/she has.

⁸³ Chatterji, op.cit, 2.

⁸⁴ H.L. Malsawma, op.cit., 128.

⁸⁵ For detailed information, see B.Lalthangliana, *History and Culture of Mizo…,*op.cit., 309-312. Also see H.L. Malsawma, …,op.cit.,125-134.

⁸⁶ Lalrinawmi Ralte, "Dance Theology", *Journal of Asian Women's Resources Centre for Culture and Theology* 19/4 (December, 2000): 36.

⁸⁷ The British authorities in Cachar dispatched a series of punitive expeditions against the Mizo raiders. The first was in 1844; under the Commander of Captain Blackwood, and because of the repeated raids, the action for expeditions by the Government took place in 1871–72; 1888–89 and 1889–90 against the Mizo. See B. C. Allen, *Gazetteers of Bengal and North East India* (New Delhi: Mittal Publications, 1979), 7; See also R. G. Woodthorpe, *The Lushai Expedition, 1871-72* (Guwahati: Spectrum Publications, 1980), 37; Also see A.S. Reid, *Chin-Lushai Land* (Calcutta: Firma KLM, 1978), 16.

⁸⁸ J.V. Hluna, *Education and Missionaries in Mizoram* (Guwahati: Spectrum Publication, 1992), 27.

⁸⁹ *Ibid.*

[90] Zairema, *God's Miracle in Mizoram* (Aizawl: Synod Press and Bookroom, 1978), 1.

[91] C.G. Verghese and R.L. Thanzawna, *A History of the Mizos,* Vol. I. (Delhi: Vikas Publishing House, 1997), 198.

[92] For more detailed information, see, A.S Reid, *Chin-Lushai Land* (Aizawl: Firma Private Limited for Tribal Research Institute Government of Mizoram, 1st Edition 1893, Reprinted, 2008), 1-13. Also see T.H. Lewin, *A Fly on the wheel* (Aizawl: Tribal Research Institute, Art &Culture Department, 2nd Reprint 2005 of First edition, 1912), 230-290.

[93] See R.L. Rokhuma, *Mizoram Zirna a Mission leh Kohhran Rawngbawlna [Mission and the Church Ministry Towards Mizoram Education]* (Lunglei: Communication Department BCM, 1988), 26.

[94] *Ibid.*

[95] *Ibid.*

[96] B. Lalthangliana, *History and Culture of Mizo...,*op.cit., 480.

[97] Under the Government of India Act of 1935, hill areas of Assam were divided into "excluded areas" and "partially excluded area." The Lushai Hill District was termed an excluded area. This implied that the Mizos were outside the direct control of the Provincial Legislature of Assam and the Superintendent represented the Viceroy of India. In fact, the sole aim of the British authorities was to retain the tribal areas on the eastern parts of India as "property of the Crown." So, the Superintendent and the Governor in Assam Province, with the blessings of the British authorities and the Parliament, kept the Lushai areas away from the popular rule, under their political agents and specially appointed Superintendents. See Chawngthanpari, *A Historical Study of the Educational Ministry of the Baptist Church of Mizoram since1950s* (Doctoral Thesis, Mysore University, 2006), 103.

[98] C.L. Hminga, op.cit., 39.

[99] Lalhruaitluanga Ralte, *Zoram Vartian [The Dawn of the Zoram]* (Aizawl: Fine Print, 2008), 193.

[100] 'Report for 1903', in *The Annual Report on BMS on Mizoram 1901-1938* (Serkawn: Mizoram Gospel Centenary Committee, BCM, 1993), 6. See also Neils et al., *Concise Dictionary of the Christian World Mission* (Nashville: Abingdon Press, 1971), 35.

[101] K. Thanzauva, comp., "The report of the Lushai Hills, 1894," in *Reports of the Foreign Mission of the Presbyterian church of Wales on Mizoram 1894-1985* (Aizawl: The Synod Literature and Publication Boards, 1997), 1.

[102] J.H. Lorrain and F.W. Savidge, "Report for 1903," in *The Annual Report on BMS on Mizoram 1901-1938* (Serkawn: Mizoram Gospel Centenary Committee, BCM, 1993), 6-7.

[103] *Ibid*

[104] Frederick S. Downs, *History of Christianity in North East India, Volume V, part 5* (Bangalore: The Church History Association of India, 2003), 190.

[105] *Ibid.*

[106] *Ibid.*

[107] *Ibid.*

[108] Lalhmuaka, *Zoram Thim ata Engah [Zoram: From Darkness to Light]* (Aizawl: The Synod Publication Board, 1988), 98. B.Lalthangliana, "A Aw b kan lo neihdan leh thu ziak lama hmasawn thu," in *Kum za lamtluanga* ['The formulation of A Aw B and the development of Our literatiure,' in *the way of Hundred Years]* (Aizawl: Mizo Centenary Celebration Organizing Committee, 1994), 64. As quoted by Lalhruaitluanga Ralte, op.cit., 208.

[109] J. Meirion LLoyd, op.cit., 262-263.

[110] The Hunterian System for the writing of proper names was developed in the 1860s by William Wilson Hunter, Director-General of Statistics for India, and published in Hunter's *Guide to the Orthography of Indian Proper Names* (Calcutta, 1871). The Government of India accepted the system with some modifications in 1872, and it was used in the official *Imperial Gazetteer of India* (1881 onwards; 24 volumes), a work initiated by Hunter. See "The Romanization of Toponyms in the Countries of South Asia" By United Nations Group Of Experts On Geographical Names Meeting of the Working Group on Romanization Systems Tallinn, 9-11 October 2006. *http://www.eki.ee/wgrs/wgr06_5.htm.* Accessed on 21st February 2011.

[111] V. Hawla, *Zoram Hmar Chan Zosapte Chanchin[The Story of Missionaries in Northern Mizoram]*(Aizawl: The Synod Bookroom, 1969), 13.

[112] J.H. Lorrain, *Dictionary…*, op.cit., viii.

[113] R.L Rokhuma,op.cit., 50.

[114] Rinchamliana, *The History Of The Mizo Bible Translation From 1897 To 1956: A Postcolonial Appraisal* (M.Th. Thesis, Senate of Serampore College [University] , 2010), 21.

[115] J. Meirion LLoyd, op.cit., 28.

[116] B. Lalthangliana, *Mizo Literature* (Aizawl: M.C. Lalrinthanga, Second edition, 2004), 118.

[117] *Ibid.,*119.

[118] *Ibid.,* 199.

[119] Pu Buanga [J.H. Lorrain], Log book, Dated 26th October, 1894.

[120] B.Lalthangliana, *Mizo Literature*, op.cit., 120.

[121] Lalnghinglova, *Zoram nghahchhan[The Foundation of Zoram]* (Aizawl: Saikungi, second edition 2000), 50.

[122] J.V. Hluna, op.cit., 2.

[123] D.E Jones, "The Report of the Lushai Hills, 1898-1899," op.cit., 3.

[124] J.V. Hluna, op.cit., 62.

[125] Resolution of 8 January, 1864; B.E.P 1864; 8 January, No. 25. As quoted By J.V. Hluna, op.cit.,62.

[126] J.V. Hluna, op.cit., 62.

[127] D.F. Glover, *set on a hill, the record of 50 years in the Lushai country* (London: Carey Press, 1944), 11.

[128] T.H. Lewin, *A Fly on the Wheel or How I helped to Govern India* (Aizawl: Tribal Research Institute, Art &Culture Department, 3nd Reprint 2005 of first edition 1912), 316.

[129] Vumson Suantak, "Common Language for Zo(Chin) people in Burma", "http://zogamnuam.com/index.php/eng/artl/220-commonlanguage.html" http://zogamnuam.com. Accessed on 17th Feb. 2010.

[130] J. Meirion LLoyd, op.cit., 28.

[131] J.V. Hluna, op.cit., 57.

[132] Aizawl Record File, No. 35G Dt. 15. 4. 1898, from Major Shakespeare, Superintendent of the Lushai Hills, to the Secretary to the Chief Commissioner of Assam. As quoted by J.V. Hluna, op.cit., 57.

[133] J.V. Hluna, op.cit, 57.

[134] J.V. Hluna, op.cit, 52-53.

[135] Chawngthanpari, op.cit., 108.

[136] J. Herbert Kane, *Understanding Christian Mission* (Grand Rapids: Baker Book House, 1974), 318.

[137] Some of the writers like J.V. Hluna put it April 2, 1894 as the date for starting the school, however, it was in April 1, 1894 according to some writers and some documents like: Lalhmuaka, *Zoram Thim ata Engah [Zoram: From Darkness to Light]*(Aizawl: The Synod Publication Board, 1988), 98. C. Lalchawimawia, Comp. *"British Rule in Mizoram Collection of Important Documents Volume I:Missionary and the Government 1891-1961* (N.p: C.Lalchawimawia, 2010), 198. Zawnga, *Mizoram Baptist Kohhran Chanchin [A Collection of Important events]*, part 1 (Serkawn: Literature Committee, 1990), 35. As quoted by Chawngthanpari, Op.cit., 108.

[138] K.L. Rokhuma, op.cit., 76.

[139] D.E Jones and Edwin Rowlands, *Reports of the Foreign Mission…*, op.cit., 19. Aizawl record File, No. 25684 dt. 27.3.1903. Letter from the D.P.I Assam to the superintendent of Lushai Hills.

[140] Data are collected from BCM Archive.

[141] Lalbiakliana, op.cit., 77.

[142] *Ibid.*

[143] Letter from Maj. Shakespear to the secretary to the Chief Commissioner of Assam, No.158G dated 20 May, 1901. As quoted by J.V. Hluna, op.cit, 77.

[144] *Ibid.*

[145] No. 12.P.I./1664 G dt. 4.3.1903 letter from the Secretary to the Chief Commissioner, to the D.P.I., Assam. As cited by J.V. Hluna, Op.cit., 65.

[146] F.W.Savidge, *The Annual Reports of BMS…*, op.cit., 12.

[147] Lalbiakliana, *Mizoram Zirna Chanchin* (Aizawl: Education Department, Mizoram, 1979), 27. See also R.L. Rokhuma, op.cit., 79.

[148] The data are collected from the statistical report of the Report of the Lushai Hills for the years 1899, 1900, 1901 and 1902, in *Reports of the Foreign Mission…*,op.cit.,

2-16. Lalhmuaka, *Zoram Zirna Chhinchhiahna [A Record of Zoram Education]* (Aizawl: The tribal Research Institute, Education Department, Mizoram, 1981), 18-19.

[149] At *Hringmual* village, Nu-i was the teacher, at *Thakthing* village Saii was the teacher and at *Rahsi Veng* Pawngi was the teacher. The three teachers worked without any salary. Though they do not follow regularity of attendant they had a number of students. In 1903, the total number of students of the three Schools was 38, during this year, the mission school also had 50 students. It was a remarkable contribution of the Mizo women in the history of Education in Mizoram. Lalhmuaka, op.cit., 113.

[150] Lalhmuaka, op.cit.,113.

[151] J.H.Lorrain, *The Annual Reports of BMS...*, op.cit., 53.

[152] J.V. Hluna, op.cit., 91

[153] J.V. Hluna, op.cit., 91

[154] D.E. Jones, *Reports of the Foreign Mission...*, op.cit., 35

[155] *Ibid.*

[156] J.H. Lorrain, *The Annual Reports of BMS...*, op.cit., 53.

[157] F.W. Savidge, The Annual Reports of BMS...,op.cit., 79.

[158] J.V. Hluna, op.cit., 93.

[159] Lalhmuaka, op.cit., 24.

[160] *Ibid.*, 24-25,

[161] F.W. Savidge, *The Annual Reports of BMS...*, op.cit., 136.

[162] D.E Jones, *Reports of the Foreign Mission...*, op.cit., 3.

[163] B.Lalthangliana, *Mizo Literature* (Aizawl: M.C. Lalrinthanga, second edition 2004), 96.

[164] Edwin Rowlands, *Reports of the Foreign Mission...*, op.cit., 10.

[165] Lower Primary Examination Result 1904 in "*Mission School Result Record Book of the Southern Lushai,*" available in photo copy at BCM Archive, Serkawn.

[166] J.V.Hluna, op.cit., 90.

[167] The three R's stands for Reading, wRiting and aRithmetic. The phrase "the three Rs" is used because each word in the phrase has a strong *R* phoneme (sound) at the beginning. The term is ironic, since someone with a firm education in the subjects would know that two of the original words do not actually begin with an *R*. The third *R* was more probably Reckoning, not as is more usually stated Rithmetic. Reckoning was a Victorian term for mental arithmetic and had been in use as such since the 14th century.

[168] Rochunga Pudaite, *The Education of the Hmar People,* (Sielmat: Indo-Burma Pioneer Mission, 1963), 72.

[169] *Kristian Tlangau,* (Monthly Journal of the Wales Mission at Aizawl) August, 1916.

[170] J.V. Hluna, op.cit., 101.

[171] J.H. Lorrain and F.W. Savidge, *The Annual Report of BMS...,*op.cit., 116.

[172] D.E. Jones, *Reports of the Foreign Mission...,* op.cit., 21.

[173] Lalhmuaka, op.cit., 31.

174 J.V. Hluna, op.cit., 100.

175 D.E Jones, *Report of the Foreign Mission...*, op.cit., 43.

176 F.W. Savidge, *The Annual Report of BMS ...*,op.cit., 78.

177 D.E. Jones, *Report of the Foreign Mission...* op.cit., 60.

178 J.H. Lorrain, *The Annual Report of BMS...*, op.cit., 209. My grandfather Awlhmunga (L) a Mission school teacher from 1944 to 1952 also told me that during their school time, they did a lot of cane and bamboo work preparing baskets, chicken coops, and many other things. Therefore, in fact, the mission school keep tried to keep up the skill of the Mizo concerning cane and bamboo works.

179 C.Lalchawimawia, op.cit., 98..

180 Jones, D.E. and Pasena. *Zirtirh Bu Thar[New Primer]*. Aijal [sic]: Loch Press, 1951, 26th edition.

181 B.Lalthangliana, *History of Mizo Literature*, op.cit., 100

182 *Ibid.*

183 *Mizo Zirtirh Bu, 1901,* 15.

184 D.E Jones: *Duhlian Zirtirh Bu* (Madrass:SPCK Press, 1921, 5th edition), 32.

185 B.Lalthangliana, *History of Mizo Literature*, op.cit., 100.

186 *Ibid.*

187 D.E Jones, *Duh-lian zirtirh Bu* (Aijal: OMF Mission Book, 1962), 57.

188 I find no textbook document with this regard but V.L. Zawnga, Pastor pensioner told me that they used to learn the name of months in a year in Mizo language. Interview with V.L. Zawnga, BCM Pastor pensioner, Aizawl, 15 September, 1910.

189 The name of the months in a year in Mizo goes like this: *Pawl Kut thla* (January), *Ramtuk thla* (February), *Vau thla* (March), *Tau Thla* (April), *Tomir thla* (May), *Nikir* (June), *Vawkhniakzawn thla* (July), *Thitin thla* (August), *Mim Kut Thla* (September), *Khuangchawi thla* (October), *Sahmulphah thla* (November), *Pawl tlak thla* (December).

190 B.Lalthangliana, *Mizo Literature...*,op.cit.,104.

191 *Ibid.*

192 *Ibid.*

193 *Ibid.*

194 J.V. Hluna, op.cit., 100.

195 One of the traditional tune song composers Lalduhawma Chakchhuak shared me that there was a negative reaction from various comers. Even in one of the Christian Weekly papers, a negative reaction to these kinds of songs is to be read a couple of times, this led him to unsubscribing this Christian Weekly paper.

196 D.E. Jones, *Report of the Foreign Mission...* op.cit., 57.

197 As quoted by Jacob Dharmaraj, *Colonialism and the Christian Mission: Postcolonial Reflection* (Delhi: ISPCK, 1993), 69.

198 *Ibid.*

[199] Aloysius Pieres, "Towards an Asian Theology of Liberation," in *Asia's Struggle for Full Humanity,* edited Virginia Fabella (New York: Orbis, 1980), 77.

[200] Lawmsanga, "A Critical Study On Christian Mission With Special Reference To Presbyterian Church Of Mizoram," (D.Th. dissertation, University Birmingham Department of Theology and Religion, January 2010), 121-122.

[201] H.W. Carter, *The Annual Report of BMS...,* op.cit., 327.

[202] *Ibid.,* 326.

[203] J.V. Hluna, Op.cit., 132-133

[204] J.V. Hluna, Op.cit., 133.

[205] *Ibid.*

[206] The five M.E. Schools were: Boys' M.E. School, Aizawl; Girls M.E. School, Aizawl; Boys' M.E. School, Serkawn Girls M.E. School, Serkawn; and Girls M.E. School, Darzo. See J.V. Hluna, op.cit., 123.

[207] Ten Middle Vernacular Schools were: Lunglei started in 1936; Sialsuk in 1944, and the remaining started in 1945 were Saitual, Bukpui, Champhai, Reiek, Sialhawk, Darzo, Hmuntlang and Tawipui. J.V. Hluna, Op.cit.,123.

[208] K.L. Rokhuma, op.cit., 189.

[209] J.V. Hluna., op.cit., 134.

[210] Mission School Result Record Book, Xerox copy, BCM Archives, Serkawn.

[211] *Ibid.*

[212] Katie Hughes, *Reports of the Foreign Mission...,*op.cit., 158.

[213] Saprawnga was an earlier educated person in Mizoram, he became a member of the India parliament in 1952, and he was elected as CEM (Chief executive member) in 1957, 1962, and in 1965 in Lushai District Council. He was a leading figure for the struggle for the establishment of high school at Lunglei.

[214] Ch. Saprawnga, *Ka zin Kawng* [My life Journey] (Aizawl: Lalkungi, reprint 2007 of 1990), 33.

[215] A.G. Mc Call, op.cit., 203.

[216] Government Census (India), as reproduced by C.L. Hminga, op.cit, 9.

[217] Interview with Sawiluaia, one of the first-generation Christian and a pensioner of BCM Pastor, Serkawn, 7 September, 2010.

[218] Lorrain, *The Annual Report of BMS...* op.cit., 105-106.

[219] Letter from J.H.Lorrain, to J. Hezlett the Superintendent of Lushai Hills, dated 13 September 1913 states: "We have a very great difficulty in the south Lushai in obtaining pupils for the girls' boarding school, we have excellent building accommodation for at least 14 or 15, but have only 3 in resident,...In the early age of the boys boarding school down here the government, in order to induce reluctant parents to allow their boys to be educated, used to grant to them exemption from enforced (*kuli*) labour all the times their sons were at school..."

[220] The letter from M. Bradshaw, Subdivisional Officer written to the superintendent of Lushai Hills, states; "With regard to para:2 Female education I am not in favor of granting Kuli awl to parents if they force their girls to go to school. We have already built up a special class by granting Kuli Awl to boys' parents who pass the Upper Primary examination. It is difficult to see why a boy who passes an examination should be exempted from all labor…" No. 548DC. Letter from M. Bradshaw Esqr, Sub-Divisional Officer, Lungleh to the Superintendent, Lushai Hills, Aizawl. Dated the 30 September 1913.

[221] The letter of the Superintendent says: "… I quite sympathize with Mr.Lorrain's desire to encourage female education but at the same time his letter shows that a considerable number of girls are learning to read and we must be careful not to force the peace. I am inclined to think that it should be possible to fill up the boarding school with girls from the village schools as female education grows more important in the case of the people. Without granting special privileges to the parents, but if not I am willing to reconsider the matter later on." Order passed on Mr Lorrain's letter dated 13 September 1913 by the Superintendent, Lushai Hills. Memo. No. Dated Aijal 20 October 1913.

[222] J.H. Lorrain, *The Annual Report of BMS…*, op.cit., 105-106.

[223] Chhunthangvunga, *Mizo leh Vai Chanchin bu* (February:1903), 7-8.

[224] C. Nunthara, *Mizoram: Society and Polity* (Delhi: Indus Publishing Company, 1996), 61.

[225] F.W Savidge, *The Annual Report of BMS…*,op.cit., 54.

[226] J.M. LLoyd, op.cit., 35.

[227] *Ibid.*

[228] *Ibid.*, 36.

[229] E. Lewis Mendus, *The Diary of Jungle Missionaries* (Aizawl : The Synod Publication Board, Reprint 1984 of the original publication Liverpool: Foreign Mission Office Presbyterian Church of Wales, 1956), 24.

[230] J.V. hluna, op.cit, 79.

[231] E. Lewis Mendus, op.cit., 23.

[232] The compiled data are collected from Government Census (India), as reproduced by C.L. Hminga, op.cit, 9. *Statistical Hand Book*, Mizoram, 1992 as reproduced by K.L. Rokhuma, op.cit., 202; Lalthansangi, "A Situational Analysis of Women in Mizoram" (A Research Report submitted to National Commission for Women' New Delhi), 26. http://ncw.nic.in/pdfreports/Gender 20Profile-Mizoram.pdf. Accessed on 7th March 2011.

[233] J. Merion Lloyd, …, op.cit., 262.

[234] V.L. Zawnga, H.S. Luaia and K. Thanchhungnunga, pensioners of the BCM pastor hold the opinion that the respect of elders in traditional Mizo Society was extremely declined in contemporary Mizo society. Personal interviewed in the month of Sept., 2010.

[235] C.Vanlawma, *Tun Kum za Chhunga Mizo Hnam puipate 1894-1994 [The Leaders of the Mizo within this hundred Years]* (Aizawl: M.C. Lalrinthanga, 1994).

[236] Lalnghinglova, Op.cit., 28.

[237] K. Thanzauva, comp., *Reports of the Foreign Mission...*, op.cit., 137.

[238] J. Herbert Lorrain and F.W. Savidge, *The Annual Reports of BMS...*op.cit., 8.

[239] K.L. Rokhuma, op.cit., 76-77.

[240] Lalnghinglova, op.cit.,18.

[241] D.E. Jones, *Reports of the Foreign Mission...*,op.cit., 13.

[242] Lalnghinlova, op.cit., 19

[243] As cited by Lalnghinglova, op.cit., 19.

[244] D.E. Jones, *Reports of the Foreign Mission...*,op.cit., 18.

[245] Lalnghinglova Ralte., *Zoram Nghahchan*, op.cit., 20.

[246] *Ibid.*

[247] C. Vanlawma, op.cit., 196.

[248] John Williams, *Reports of the Foreign Mission...*, op.cit ., 89.

[249] This Brief account of Pasena is reproduced from C. Vanlawma, op.cit., 198.

[250] Text book prepared by Pasena were *Zirtan Bu* (the beginner), *Zirtirh Bu* (the Lushais Premier), *Zirtirh Bu Thar* (New Lushai Premier), *Mizoram chanchin* (the story of Mizoram), Assam Ram chanchin (Brief account of Assam), *India ram chanchin* (The brief account of India or Geography of India), *Sap ṭawng ZirnaBu* (English Learner) Khawvel thu (the story of the world). He also made a great contribution in Mizo Bible translation. See, C. Vanlawma, op.cit., 198.

[251] *Ibid.*

[252] Lalchhinga. *Mizo Kristian Kohhran; A Chanchin hmasa lam leh Presbytery neih Hnulamte 1894 1939 [Mizo Christian Church: The story of the Beginning and After The formation of Presbyterian 1894-1930]*, (Aizawl: L.M. Press, 1996), 14.

[253] J. Merion Llyod, op.cit., 109,146.

[254] Lalchhinga, op.cit., 14.

[255] Lalnghinglova Ralte, op.cit., 21-22.

[256] *Ibid.*, 21.

[257] J. Merion Llyod, op.cit., 146.

[258] Marina Ngursangzeli, "The role of The Early Mizo Mission School Teachers" Role in Witnessing to Christ. A paper presented at the CMS (Centre for Mission Studies) Consultation on "Witnessing to Christ in Diverse Contexts," at the Union Biblical Seminary, Pune, January 12–14, 2010.

[259] J. Merion Llyod, op.cit., 146.

[260] D.E. Jones letter written on 18 May 1911 as cited by J. Merion Llyod, op.cit., 147.

[261] Frederick S. Downs, "Christian Conversion Movements among the Hills tribe of North Easr India in the Nineteenth and Twentieth Centuries" in *Religion in South Asia*, edited by G.A. Oddie (New Delhi: Manahor Publication, Second Revised Edition 1991), 155.

[262] As quoted by Frederick S. Downs, op.cit, 197.

[263] Frederick S. Downs, op.cit., 197.

[264] J.H.Lorrain, *The Annual Reports of BMS...*, op.cit., 113.

[265] *Sih* is a small spring that generally rises in muddy soil, the ground remains damp all the dry season, and water is generally warm and often brackish, and is therefore much frequented by wild animal. A spring is believed to be haunted by evil spirits. J.H. Lorrain, *Dictionary...*, op.cit., 27.

[266] T*uivamit* is a small pool of water found in the jungle not usually far from a stream. To have a jhum near such pool is considered unlucky.

[267] All the English translations are taken from J.H. Lorrain, *Dictionary...*, op.cit.

[268] It was believed that the evil spirit is fond of passing through the saddle of the hill; therefore, it was believed that the saddle of the hill was not suitable for construction of house and was afraid of staying nearby it.

[269] *Keptuam is* the name of a large moth. This name appears to be applied to more than one species of gigantic moth, which in the olden days were regarded as superstitious, it being considered exceedingly unlucky even to set eyes upon one. J.H. Lorrain, *Dictionary...*, op.cit., 245.

[270] *Thingsairua* is the name given to a tree having a curious complete loop in each branches. This is formed by two of the branches after being separate lower down joining together. Such a tree is said to be haunted by evil spirit and therefore the place where it grows is considered unlucky for jhuming purposes. J.H. Lorrain, *Dictionary...*, op.cit., 467.

[271] *Thingzungkai* is the name given to the root of a tree crossing a stream supposed to be used as a bridge by evil spirit. J.H. Lorrain, *Dictionary...*, op.cit., 469.

[272] *Thinghlang* is a tree the branches of which have grown across one another in such a way as to form a fancied resemblance to a bier or in which a branch has grown and become reunited to the stem higher up. Such a tree is said to be haunted and it is therefore considered unlucky to jhum, the land near it. If a jhum is made, a sacrifice is necessary to appease the evil spirit. J.H. Lorrain, *Dictionary...*, op.cit., 465.

[273] *Fangfar* is a Stalactite, also the constant dropping of water from a rock or from a tree, this is regarded by the Mizo as haunted by evil spirit. J.H. Lorrain, *Dictionary...*, op.cit.,133.

[274] See footnote No. 266.

[275] B. Lalthangliana, *History and culture of Mizo...*,op.cit., 562.

[276] Z.T. Sangkhuma, 'I have seen Keptuam' *VanglainiDaily, News Paper* (Aizawl), 1 September, 2010, 4.

[277] Zairema, *Kan Bible* Hi [Our Bible] (Kolkata: Swapna Printing Works (P) Ltd., 2003), 183.

[278] D.E. Jones, *Reports of the Foreign Mission...*, op.cit., 9.

[279] F.W. Savidge, *The Annual Report of BMS...*,op.cit., 136.

[280] Lalchhinga, op.cit., 14.

[281] Lalhmuaka, op.cit., 30.

[282] Donna Strom, op.cit., 55- 56.

²⁸³ *Kelmei* is literally a goat's tail used in a sacrifice, which is worn suspended by a string round, the neck of a person for whom the animal was offered. When not so worn, it is kept carefully. To lose this, precious token or charm is regarded by the owner as a major misfortune likely to result in sickness or even death, unless another goat is quickly offered in sacrifice. A *Kelmei* is never parted with by its owner unless he has decided to abandon his animistic belief and embrace the Christian faith.

²⁸⁴ D.E. Jones, *Reports of the Foreign Mission* …,op.cit., 13.

²⁸⁵ Zairema, *God's Miracle in Mizoram…*, op.cit., 29.

²⁸⁶ E.L. Mendus, *The Diary of the Jungle…*, op.cit., 118.

²⁸⁷ P.C. Lalhmuaka, op.cit., 14.

²⁸⁸ *Ibid.*, 159.

²⁸⁹ Saiaithanga, *Mizo Kohhran Chanchin [The account of the Mizo Church]* (Mizo District, Assam: The Regional Theological Literature Committee, 1969), 14.

²⁹⁰ E.L. mendus, *The Diary of a Jungle…*, op.cit., 55.

²⁹¹ E.L. mendus, *The Diary of a Jungle…*, op.cit., 82.

²⁹² Presbytery Minute, Aijal April 22/1910.

²⁹³ *Ibid.*

²⁹⁴ See the statistic provided in the first part of this chapter. The percentage of Christian in 1961 was more than 85%, the remaining 25% (average) of the population were not Christian. Those non-Christians were mostly the Chakmas and other tribes in Mizoram. Therefore, the general understanding of the Christians population among the Mizo was 100%. But due to the population of other tribes in Mizoram, it cannot be 100% of Christian's population in Mizoram.

²⁹⁵ E.L. mendus, *The Diary of a Jungle…*, op.cit., 82.

²⁹⁶ *Ibid.*

²⁹⁷ Lawmsanga, "A Critical Study On Christian Mission With Special Reference To Presbyterian Church Of Mizoram,"…op.cit., 128. See also B. Lalthangliana, History and culture…opcit., 561.

²⁹⁸ *Ibid.* 561.

²⁹⁹ Cited by Lawmsanga, "A Critical Study On Christian Mission With Special Reference To Presbyterian Church Of Mizoram,"…op.cit.,127-128. from B.Lalthangliana, *History of Mizo Literature…*,op.cit., 113-114.

³⁰⁰ C.L. Hminga, op.cit., 291.

³⁰¹ R.M. Agarwal, *The Mizo on the Cross-road, Mizoram Today* (Vol. I. No. I, August, 1974), [An Illustrated Quarterly, Published by Govt. of Mizoram] :10, cited by Ibid.

³⁰² H.S. Luaia, *Hmanlai Mizo Khawsak dan…*, op.ct., 13.

³⁰³ B. Lalthangliana, *History and Culture of Mizo…*, op.cit., 587.

³⁰⁴ In 1914, the name "*Krista Tlangau*" was changed into "*Kristian Tlangau.*" Lalnghinglova, *Zoram Nghahchhan…*, op.cit., 126.

[305] B. Lalthangliana, *History and Culture of Mizo...*, op.cit., 588.

[306] *Ibid.*, 591.

[307] Interview with V.L Zawnga, BCM Pastor Pensioner, Aizawl, 25 October, 2011.

[308] C.L. Hminga, op.cit., 296.

[309] *Ibid.*, 296.

[310] http://centralyma.org.in an officail website of Young Mizo Association, Accessed on 3 March 2011.

[311] In 1899, out of the 56 pupils in the only school at Aizawl, there were only 6 girls. In 1950, the total number of girl students was 2063 out of the total students of 5943. In 1952, there were already 2296 girl students out of the total students of 5604. The statistic records are collected from K. Thanzauva, comp., *Reports of the Foreign Mission...*, op.cit. 1ff.

[312] The data are reproduced from Lalthansangi, op.cit., 39.

[313] For more information on women situation in Mizoram, visit http://ncw.nic.in/pdfreports/Gender 20Profile-Mizoram.pdf. Lalthansangi, "A Situational Analysis of Women in Mizoram" (A report submitted to National Commission for Women' New Delhi).

[314] D.E. Jones, *Reports of the Foreign Mission ...*, op.cit., 19.

[315] R.L. Hnuni was ordained as a Church Minister by the Assembly of the Baptist Church of Mizoram in 2011. She is the first woman ordained by the Churches in Mizoram.

[316] M.S. Dawngliana, "Ministry of BCM Relief & Development Department," *BCM Conpendium* (Serkawn, Lunglei: Centenary Committee BCM, 2003), 83.

[317] A.G. Mc Call, op.cit., 205.

[318] *Ibid.*

[319] A.G. Mc Call, op.cit., 206.

[320] C. Nunthara, op.cit., 38.

[321] *Ibid.*

[322] In 1909, the Aizawl Bazar (market) was opened by Major Cole, the Superintendent of the hills. Small shops thrived to grow around the bazaar areas. The gradual spread of monetary transaction gave impetus to small trade in all sorts of local consumption goods. Goods were transported from Silchar (Assam) through the river *tlawng* and the Aizawl Silchar road. See C. Nunthara, op.cit., 38.